Volume III

CLINICAL AND MEDICAL HYPNOTHERAPY

Volume III

CLINICAL AND MEDICAL HYPNOTHERAPY

HYPNOANESTHESIA, PAIN CONTROL, AND IMPROVED HEALTH

Dr. Gisella Zukausky, DCH,BS,CHt,CtHA

VOLUME III CLINICAL AND MEDICAL HYPNOTHERAPY
HYPNOANESTHESIA, PAIN CONTROL, AND IMPROVED HEALTH

iUniverse books may be ordered through booksellers or by contacting:

iUniverse
1663 Liberty Drive
Bloomington, IN 47403
www.iuniverse.com
1-800-Authors (1-800-288-4677)

Because of the dynamic nature of the Internet, any web addresses or links contained in this book may have changed since publication and may no longer be valid. The views expressed in this work are solely those of the author and do not necessarily reflect the views of the publisher, and the publisher hereby disclaims any responsibility for them.

Any people depicted in stock imagery provided by Thinkstock are models, and such images are being used for illustrative purposes only.
Certain stock imagery © Thinkstock.

ISBN: 978-1-4917-7855-5 (sc)
ISBN: 978-1-4917-7856-2 (e)

Print information available on the last page.

iUniverse rev. date: 05/06/2016

TABLE OF CONTENTS

HYPNOSIS: A VALUABLE TOOL FOR ANESTHESIA, PAIN MANAGEMENT, AND IMPROVED HEALTH

Dr. Gisella Zukausky, D.C.H.,B.S.,

There are many misconceptions regarding hypnosis. Hypnosis is a daydream state. This is any time you are not making yourself think. When you on the other hand are making yourself think you are using your conscious mind. When you are not making any effort to think such as when you are daydreaming, than you are in your subconscious mind. We refer to this as being hypnotized.

Because of what is shown in movies and TV there are many myths. When one is in their subconscious mind or in hypnosis. For one thing they are not unconscious or asleep. Sometimes they may appear very relaxed as though they are asleep. Everything is heard and felt. Although an individual is more suggestible when in their subconscious mind they are still free to reject anything that they would find unacceptable. Individuals can lie or refuse to answer questions when in a subconscious state. They can open their eyes if they wish and walk out.

I am often asked if people who are taking part in stage hypnosis are doing all those crazy things aren't they being controlled by the hypnotist? No they are not. First of all the hypnotist does not just pick these people out of the audience. These individuals have volunteered to be a part of this. They know full well they will be asked to do crazy things. They are being good sports about it and they think it will be entertaining and fun. Almost without exception they will be aware of what they are being asked to do. As long as they do not find it objectionable they will do what is asked in their most creative way.

When one understands how the mind works and that we can create our own reality by continually focusing on a given thought it will happen. This is what we refer to as the power of positive thinking. Norman Vincent Peal, a minister, wrote **THE POWER OF POSITIVE THINKING** clearly explains this. He explains some techniques how to focus the mind to achieve any goal. This same method can be used whether it be for our career, personal desires, or health.

Our conscious mind does all the reasoning and thinking. Our subconscious does not. The subconscious only takes in information we hear, see, experience, or continually focus on. Then our subconscious mind begins to react to this information. It does not matter if the information that we have programmed into this mental computer is correct or real. It will still respond to it as though it is correct or real. I do demonstrations when I give lectures to show how the subconscious does this. It is important to keep in mind that this is exactly what happens when we use the power of positive thinking. What we focus on becomes our reality, whether it be positive thoughts or negative thoughts. If we are positive we will fail, we probably will. On the other hand the more we are focused on being positive that we will succeed the more likely we will. Realizing how the mind does this it then can be used in many areas in our life, physical, mental, and spiritual.

1

Our subconscious mind is the part of our mind that controls everything, not only our behavior, likes, and dislikes, but also our health. So what ever we focus on or keep thinking or saying to ourselves will eventually happen. This is what the power of positive thinking is all about. What we don't realize is that negative thinking and focus will also come to pass. The reason that we can get our subconscious mind to do what we focus on is because it is not the part of our mind that reasons and thinks. It just programs whatever we focus on or think and then like a robot will react to it as though it is really happening.

Hypnosis can be used as anesthesia for dental work, medical procedures, operations, and improving health, as well as having the patient respond favorably and quickly to the doctors treatments. I used self hypnosis for anesthesia when I had a root canal done. The dentist drilled for 45 minutes. I have taught others self anesthesia for dental work, painless child birth, and for operations. When hypnosis is used there is practically no bleeding, and healing is at least six times faster. For example: before an operation it helps the patient to be more relaxed and therefore requiring less medication before an operation. It can be used during an operation, thereby greatly reducing the amount of anesthesia and perhaps not requiring any. It almost eliminates bleeding, as demonstrated on a video I show my class. The video shows a doctor hypnotizing his patient and doing a cesarean operation on the expectant mother. This video was shown recently on TV. He had also told the mother while still in a state of hypnosis that her milk would come in on the second day instead of the usual third day. It did. Post operative symptoms are eliminated or greatly reduced. This also again decreases the need for medications.

Anyone with pain can be taught, usually in the first session, to eliminate or at least reduce their chronic pain. The amazing thing is that with hypnosis pain can be eliminated or greatly reduced by just learning how to focus the mind. Most people can reduce or eliminate their pain in less than a minute. Occasionally there is an individual who is unable to do this. Further Regression therapy with hypnosis can get to the cause and resolve it, whatever is preventing relief.

Much has been published including in medical journals on improved health with using what is referred to as Imagery. Here again it can be done without the need to be hypnotized, and just learning how to use the imagination in focusing the mind or picturing in our mind the healing taking place. Bernie S. Siegel, M.D. who is a cancer specialist has written **LOVE MEDICINE AND MIRACLES**, also, **PEACE, LOVE AND HEALING.** These are two excellent books and are must reading for medical professionals, anyone who ever gets ill or knows of others who are. This works for anything. Dr. Siegel's success rate is way above the national average.

Dr. Gisella Zukausky is certified to teach Hypnosis for Anesthesia, Pain Management, and Improved Health.

She is a Certified Clinical Hypnotherapist with the International Medical, Dental, and Hypnotherapy Association. She has been in private practice since 1986, and is the founder and director of Midwest Training Institute of Hypnosis in Fort Wayne, IN. She has taught in the Philippines and in India as well as many Conferences in the United States.

She is often asked to be a guest lecturer at colleges and universities in the Fort Wayne area and abroad.

Gisella had a television series on the local access channel in Fort Wayne, IN called Hypnosis For Quality Living. She has been interviewed for television and radio programs internationally, and for a number of magazines and newspaper articles in this country as well as abroad.

Dr. Zukausky was on the faculty at St. John's Institute in Louisiana. The American Directory of Who's Who in Executives & Businesses approves Dr. Gisella L. Zukausky, C.Ht., Ct.H.A. for inclusion in the 1998-1999 edition.

She was nominated "Woman Of The Year – 2005" to the American Biographical Institute by its worldwide research Board of over ten thousand members for inclusion in "The International Directory of Experts and Expertise."

Zukausky has been nominated for 2008 Commemorative Medal by the Woman of the Year Board of International Research for her dedication toward her profession and the notable example she has set for her peers and community by the American Biographical Institute.

INFORMATION YOU SHOULD KNOW

Dr. James Braid, a prominent Manchester, England surgeon, is considered to be the father of the scientific evaluation of hypnosis for writing "Doctrine Of Suggestion".

George Q Colton, an itinerant chemist, gave an exhibition in Hartford, Connecticut on December 11, 1844. Mr Colton used laughing gas to place subjects appearing in his stage show in a hypnotic state. During the show a young man under the influence of laughing gas stumbled against a chair and badly bruised his legs. Mr. Colton terminated the hypnotic trance and sent the young man back to his seat in the audience.

Aaron A Moss D.D.S., and a group of colleagues banded together to spread the gospel of hypnosis in dentistry. In order to dispel the superstition and myths about clinical hypnosis, Dr. Moss coined the term hypnodontics.

In 1955, The British Medical Association approved the use of hypnosis for the treatment of psychoneurosis and for the anesthesia during surgery for childbirth

On September 13, 1958, the Council on Mental Health of the America Medical Association recommended; in view of our increasing knowledge, hypnosis instruction be included in the curricula of medical schools and post graduate training centers. In 1961 the AMA gave further approval for the use of clinical hypnotherapy by recommending a minimum of 144 hours of training in hypnotherapy for student physicians and medical doctors.

ACCEPTING & UTILIZING

How to shift them to be more accepting...
"I will help you to achieve what you want."
"What is it you want?"
"I can help you with that?"

1955 British Medical Association approved use of hypnosis for treatment of psychoneurosis and anesthesia for surgery and child birth.

September 13, 1958 Council on Mental Health of American Medical Association recommended hypnosis be included in medical school training

1961 AMA gave approval for clinical Hypnotherapy

1700's Anto Mesmer tubs of water with rods etc. cures spontaneous remission

Sigmund Freud developed psycho analytical theory

1843 Dr Jones Brea started mesmerizing eliminating rods than had them close eyes. Called in hypnosis- Monidism narrow in one idea or thought such as watching pendulum, "listening to my voice", etc.

After WW2, Menninger Clinic in Kansas

1950's Catholic said OK for medical "has to do with the mind" Milton Erickson psychologist had polio as child used imagery for himself (NLP), metaphors.

THREE MOST COMMON REASONS FOR ILLNESS

1. Physical or emotional stress for long periods of time.

2. Self guilt.

3. To manipulate (getting something you wouldn't otherwise get, such as attention etc. This is not consciously realized by the patient most of the time).

One must always be careful what they are thinking or saying. The subconscious mind is always listening and filing away in their subconscious mind what you say and think.

How many people do you hear say:

"Their a pain in the neck."
"Get off my back."
"I can't carry anymore responsibility."
"Their a pain in the butt (ass)."
"My heart bleeds for them."
"My heart breaks for them."
"I've got a _bad_ leg (arm, shoulder, etc.)"
and on and on

What you keep focusing on is programmed into the sub-conscious mind and will eventually cause it. The Power Of Positive Thinking works for good or bad.

I read in a doctors journal that 80% of doctors think that illness even infectious diseases are psychosomatic.

USES FOR MEDICAL HYPNOSIS

Hypnodontics, Hypnoanesthesia, Painless Childbirth, Improved Health, Reduce or Eliminate Chronic Pain

DIFFERENT METHODS TO USE MEDICAL HYPNOSIS

Pain and Anxiety
Imagery for pain management and improved health
Regression remembering before they had pain
Disassociation
Impulse Control:
Aversion techniques – you'll gag if you... Not to be used if not good self image or medical reason not to. Patient seldom responds to negative suggestions. If this is a problem it is best to have Regression Therapy to get to what is causing it worked out and resolved first.
Waking Hypnosis – lock your mind around a given idea and accept it.

QUESTIONS TO ASK THE CLIENT

What do you get from this illness that you would not have otherwise? How is your life different now that you have this illness? (See if they have more done for them or get more attention etc.)

How much do you need this illness?
OK, now make the changes so you can release the illness and not need it any more.

Dr. Don Colbertt wrote the book <u>Deadly Emotions</u>. In this book he explains that all physical problems are caused by emotions. He details how each negative emotion affects our bodies and what kind of chemical change happens and how it then leads to what kind of illness.

It already is known that worry and stress can cause ulcers, back problems, migraines, allergies, etc.

Tell the cancer patients all stress create glandular events.

An example is the glandular reaction when they are asked to close their eyes and imagine sucking on a sour lemon. It causes us to salivate.

Inform the patient's family they should treat the patient the same way as when they are well. Otherwise the patient could possibly not get well or even die as not to disappoint them or be treated differently.

Depression is caused from feelings of helplessness and hopelessness. These feelings cause chemical changes to occur in the body, and can eventually lead to death.

Help the patient to feel better about themselves, and build their confidence. (You can give them a Confidence CD to listen to each day.)

I always do Regression Therapy on my patients that come to me with physical problems. This directs their subconscious mind under hypnosis to go to the incidents that have caused the problem and then we resolve those negative feelings and emotions that were never resolved. When all is resolved from the past they get well. The subconscious mind then can reverse itself and cause the body to return to wellness. I have had terminally ill people get well with regression therapy after resolving all the feelings and emotions that had caused their illness.

Patients usually have tension. Help them to find a way to release it. Give them a relaxing and sleep CD. I also teach them how to do Anchoring (see next chapter) which is a technique that removes any bad feelings and emotions usually in less than a minute. More traumatic emotions and events could take up to twenty (20) minutes to resolve and get rid of. Once the the bad feelings and emotions are totally gone they never come back.

<u>Sunlight</u> for at least 30 minutes a day (not in the hottest part of the day) is very good for the patients wellness.

Tell the patient to make the treatment a good friend that is helping them, and to give it a name. Have them tell their friend (treatment) to knock the bad cells block off, and tell their bodies they don't need this, they don't want this, and to make this go away now, never to return. Have them close their eyes and imagine the healing taking place in their bodies. A man who had cancer imagined the good cells as army tanks (he had served in WW2 in the tank core) and directed the tanks to go and attack and eliminate the German army which was the cancer. In less than three months he no longer had cancer. The reason this works is that the sub-conscious mind is like a computer. It takes in information and since it doesn't think like our conscious mind does, it will react to what we keep focusing on as though it is real.

I have had the cancer patient imagine little fire trucks going throughout their veins and then their bowels to put out the fire after chemo therapy. For the fire in their stomach I had them imagine a crew of little men with buckets of pink liquid that they direct to coat the stomach with to stop the burning. You can have them decide whatever way they want to imagine otherwise.

I have even done this over the phone with great success to eliminate patients pain. I have already programed them before hand to be able to go into hypnotic trance by giving them the Post-Hypnotic Suggestion that when I hypnotize them from now on all I will need to do is have them close their eyes and when I count from ten (10) to one (1) that by the time I count to one they will have multiplied their relaxation so rapidly that they will be in a nice comfortable state of hypnosis. By doing this at the end of the first session you work on them this will happen and save a great deal of time hypnotizing them in the future.

This way you can help more patients instead of having to go to them every time. Once you have them conditioned and have their confidence it is easy.

You can also help them to sleep this way as well. To help them go to sleep when they are unable to take them for a walk through the wood or along the sea shore etc. Suggest, if they aren't afraid of the water they are going on a little sail boat with you into your secret cove etc. Then give suggestions that they will have a deep wonderful night sleep with happy and contented dreams.

If they need to void or someone has to do a procedure on them they will open their eyes and when it is done they will close their eyes and again go into a deep wonderful sleep.

Call the nurses station if they are in the hospital, or whoever is attending them before you start doing this to let them know what you are doing and tell them what you did. That they are to avoid talking unnecessarily to the patient because they will still be in hypnosis and too much talk can bring them out. It should take only 10 to 15 minutes to do this to the patient working with them on the phone. This has worked very successfully for me.

If the patient had an accident have them keep repeating it when in hypnosis till they say they do not feel any feelings or emotions connected with the accident. Using <u>Time Distortion</u> is the quickest, least traumatic way, and easiest way to do this.

This is done by saying, "I WANT YOUR INNER MIND TO PLAY THIS WHOLE EVENT ON FAST FORWARD EVERY SECOND, SO THAT AT THE END OF EACH MINUTE YOU WILL HAVE RELIVED THE EVENT 60 TIMES. NOW BEGIN."

At the end of two (2) minutes ask them to go back to the event at regular speed and tell you if there are any feelings or emotions, even a tiny bit left at all. As long as they still feel a tiny bit repeat the time distortion till it is entirely gone. This is a very rapid and painless way for them to do it. The healing is much more rapid if this is done right after the accident. If the accident was a long time ago it is still advisable as holding in any feelings and emotions that were never released could cause problems physically even years later.

One way to eliminate or reduce their pain is to tell them,

IMAGINE THE SHAPE AND SIZE OF YOUR PAIN, AND GIVE IT A COLOR. NOW IMAGINE AN OPENING IN THE CENTER OF ALL THIS DISCOMFORT AND IT ALL STARTING TO COME OUT. VAPORIZING IN THE AIR LIKE STEAM OUT OF A KETTLE. (if they have the pain in their back and they are laying down or in a chair have them imagine it is soaking into the chair or bed.)

YOU BEGIN TO NOTICE THAT AS MORE AND MORE COME OUT AND VAPORIZE INTO THE AIR LIKE STEAM OUT OF STEAM KETTLE THE SHAPE AND SIZE IS GETTING SMALLER AND SMALLER. DO YOU NOTICE THAT? NOW KEEP NOTICING MORE AND MORE COME OUT TILL IT IS ALL OUT. IF THERE IS SOME REASON YOUR SUBCONSCIOUS MIND FEELS YOU NEED SOME OF THE DISCOMFORT AT LEAST MOST OF IT WILL COME OUT. LET ME KNOW WHEN YOU HAVE ALL OF IT OR AS MUCH AS YOU CAN OUT.
(When they say it is out or mostly out then say.)

AS YOU THINK ABOUT THE AREA IN YOUR (LOWER BACK/ or whatever the part of the body is) THOSE THOUGHTS CAUSE THAT PART TO FEEL COMFORTABLE, LEAVING THIS AREA OF YOUR BACK FEELING COMFORTABLE, PLEASANT AND RELAXED.

To save time remember at the end of their very first session to give them a post hypnotic suggestions that when you ask them to close their eyes the next time and count backwards from 10 to 1 they will be in the deepest relaxation they have ever felt.

You can also say if you feel they are a devout believer: "Before we can get well we must feel we want GOD more than to be healed."

Being afraid of the illness is worse than the illness.

I build a report with my patients on their first session. I ask them on the first session if we can start with me saying a prayer for God's guidance. Everyone in all my years of practice has said yes. In fact it makes most people feel more at ease and comfortable.

Dr. B. Siegel says to visualize 15 minutes at a time, 3 times a day. He says to get relaxed and then to imagine the healing taking place. To see or imagine the self healing, being active, happy, and loving themselves and others. These emotions increase the immune system.

Telling oneself during the day many times that you don't need and don't want the illness. Tell your body what you want it to do. Saying that you want it to go away, to go away now, and to never return. Imagine how the healing is taking place.

When you teach the patient to visualize or to imagine their healing or to tell their body what to do, they must <u>always make their statements in the present tense</u> as the subconscious mind deals only in the present tense. Therefore, avoid using words such as "will". This word implies that it will happen in the future. As far as the subconscious mind is concerned the future never happens.

It is also important to instruct them to use only positive words if they want to get well. Such as:

MY BODY FEELS BETTER AND BETTER EVERY HOUR.

Instead of:

MY BODY DOES NOT FEEL ANY PAIN AND NO LONGER ILL. This is still focusing on the negative and the subconscious will not cause improvement but will only be reinforcing the pain and illness.

For example: if the patient has cancer they may see it as black dots and the cancer fighting cells as pack man going over to the cancer dots and gobbling them up.

WHAT ARE THE ADVANTAGES
FOR HYPNO-ANESTHESIA?

1. Reduce stress and fears by making them more relaxed before the operation. This reduces the need for medication.

2. Bleeding is almost nill because the veins suture them self shut.

3. Always give suggestions for rapid healing. Sometimes the healing is as much as 6 to 10 times faster.

4. Always give suggestions for comfort after the operation. This reduces the need for medication.

5. Always give suggestions for sound and comfortable sleep.

HELPFUL INFORMATION

If you have the client in the Esdaile Coma state it is so deep that you do not have to tell the client that they will feel no pain and only good comfortable feelings.

They will automatically be in a state of anesthesia. This state is best for long operations where the patient has to stay in one position for a long period of time. They will remain in whatever position they are placed. They will not move when you ask them to in this state. Only in the depth of Somnambulism which is a lighter state will the patient move if you tell them to. In this Somnambulism you must tell them that they will feel no pain, only good comfortable feelings, otherwise they will not be in an anesthesia state. If you don't tell them they will only feel good comfortable feelings they will feel pain.

If you want to get the patient in the Esdaile Coma state you do both the Somnambulism script and the Esdaile script together. You may have to hypnotize the patient a number of times for them to achieve that deep a state.

Also, the patient will not come out of the Esdaile Coma state when you try to emerge them unless you say to them, "IF YOU EVER WANT TO BE THIS RELAXED AGAIN YOU WILL OPEN YOUR EYES AND BE COMPLETELY AWAKE AND ALERT WHEN I COUNT FROM ONE TO FIVE." Then very slowly count up from one to five.

Is of course very important that you know how to recognize when they are in the Esdaile state if you wanted to put them that deep.

SOMNAMBULISM SCRIPT

(Get eye closure and do deepening. do not read out loud what is in parentheses. That is for your information only.)

I WOULD LIKE YOU TO PICK A SPOT ON THE CEILING ABOVE EYE LEVEL.

YOU MAY CLOSE YOUR EYES ANY TIME YOU LIKE. I AM GOING TO COUNT FROM FIVE DOWN TO ONE. AS I DO, YOUR EYES WILL BECOME HEAVIER AND HEAVIER, MORE AND MORE TIRED. IF THEY ARE STILL OPEN ON THE COUNT OF ONE, *THEN JUST ALLOW THEM TO CLOSE AND RELAX.*

FIVE, YOUR EYES ARE GETTING HEAVIER AND HEAVIER. FOUR, YOUR EYES ARE GETTING MORE AND MORE TIRED. THREE, YOUR EYES ARE GETTING DROOPIER AND DROWSIER. TWO, YOUR EYES ARE GETTING VERY HEAVY AND TIRED. ONE, *NOW JUST ALLOW YOUR EYES TO RELAX AND CLOSE.*

I'D LIKE YOU TO TAKE A NICE LONG DEEP BREATH IN THROUGH YOUR NOSE AND LET IT OUT THROUGH YOUR MOUTH. GOOD. NOW TAKE ANOTHER NICE LONG DEEP BREATH IN THROUGH YOUR NOSE AND LET IT ALSO OUT THROUGH YOUR MOUTH, EXCELLENT. NOW TAKE A VERY LONG DEEP BREATH AND HOLD IT......... NOW LET IT OUT THROUGH YOUR MOUTH. YOU CAN FEEL YOURSELF GETTING MORE AND MORE RELAXED. WITH EVERY BREATH YOU EXHALE YOU CONTINUE TO GO DEEPER AND DEEPER RELAXED.

ANY SOUNDS YOU HEAR IN THIS ROOM OR OUTSIDE OF THIS ROOM JUST REASSURES YOU EVERYTHING IS NORMAL, AND THEREFORE, YOU FIND EVERY SOUND JUST GUIDES YOU DEEPER AND DEEPER RELAXED. IN A MOMENT I AM GOING TO ASK YOU TO OPEN AND CLOSE YOUR EYES. WHEN I DO THIS YOU ARE GOING TO BE ABLE TO RELAX TWICE AS MUCH AS YOU ARE NOW. OPEN YOUR EYES AND CLOSE YOUR EYES. VERY GOOD. ....OPEN YOUR EYES AND CLOSE YOUR EYES............OPEN YOUR EYES AND CLOSE YOUR EYES.

RELAX AND LET YOURSELF BE COVERED WITH A BEAUTIFUL BLANKET OF RELAXATION ALL THE WAY DOWN TO YOUR TOES. YOU WILL GO DEEPLY RELAXED BUT YOU WILL NOT GO TO SLEEP. *(REPEAT)*

(complement them how good they are doing).

NOW PHYSICALLY YOU HAVE ALL THE RELAXATION WE NEED. WE WANT YOUR MIND TO BE JUST AS RELAXED AS YOUR BODY IS, SO I WANT YOU TO START COUNTING WHEN I TELL YOU TO...NOT BEFORE, FROM 100 TO 97. AS YOU COUNT YOU WILL GO TWICE AS RELAXED AS THE NUMBER BEFORE. NOW

THE INTERESTING THING THAT WILL HAPPEN IS AS YOU INCREASE YOUR RELAXATION….THOSE NUMBERS JUST RELAX RIGHT OUT OF YOUR MIND. WANT IT TO HAPPEN AND JUST LET IT HAPPEN. ONLY YOU CAN MAKE IT HAPPEN.

NOW START COUNTING OUT LOUD OR SILENTLY VERY SLOWLY. *(100)* DEEPER AND DEEPER RELAXED AND START LETTING GO OF THE NUMBERS. *(99)* GOING DEEPER

AND DEEPER…..LET THE NUMBERS DISAPPEAR OUT OF YOUR MIND….JUST AS THOUGH YOU ARE TURNING OFF A SWITCH IN YOUR MIND. *(98)* DOUBLE YOUR RELAXATION AGAIN AND WATCH THE NUMBERS DISAPPEAR…..*(97) (PAUSE)*

IF YOU FEEL THERE ARE ANY OTHER NUMBERS THERE, IMAGINE ERASING THEM ALL OFF AT ONE TIME. NOD YOUR HEAD WHEN YOU FEEL THEY ARE ALL GONE.

(when they nod, continue).

TRY TO MOVE YOUR LEFT ARM, *(AS SOON AS THEY TWITCH SAY)* GOOD STOP TRYING. THE MORE DIFFICULT YOU FIND IT IS TO MOVE, IT ONLY MEANS THAT YOU ARE GOING DEEPER RELAXED. NOW TRY TO MOVE YOUR RIGHT ARM, GOOD STOP TRYING. TRY TO MOVE YOUR LEFT LEG, FINE STOP TRYING. TRY TO MOVE YOUR RIGHT LEG, GOOD STOP TRYING. TRY TO OPEN YOUR EYES, OK STOP TRYING.

(This is how you do the convincer test after you have hypnotized them so they have proof that they really are hypnotized. It is very important to prove to your client that they are not just sitting in the chair with their eyes closed or they will not give much credit to your therapy when they leave.

If they only twitched their arms and legs, and didn't open their eyes when you told them to try, then say the following because they would be ready for surgery. <u>All they need for them to feel no pain is to just tell them they won't.</u>)

YOU FEEL NO DISCOMFORT IN YOUR BODY….ONLY GOOD WONDERFUL COMFORTABLE FEELINGS. THERE IS NO DISCOMFORT IN YOUR BODY. ONLY GOOD FEELINGS THROUGHOUT YOUR BODY. THERE IS NO DISCOMFORT ANYWHERE IN YOUR BODY….ONLY GOOD COMFORTABLE FEELINGS THROUGHOUT YOUR ENTIRE BODY.

(Slowly start to pinch the fleshy part of their skin between your thumb and index finger till you are pinching it hard with your nails. Now as you are still pinching raise their hand up to their eyes with your other hand and say,)

*N*OW OPEN YOUR EYES AND YOU WILL SEE HOW HARD I PINCHED YOU. YOU'R HAND IS IN A STATE OF ANESTHESIA. (let go now of the pinch so they can see).

(If they are not deep enough in Somnambulism so they lifted up their arms and legs, and opened their eyes, they would feel pain unless you do and say the following:)

I'M GOING TO STROKE YOUR LEFT/RIGHT HAND. WITH EVERY STROKE YOUR HAND GETS NUMBER AND NUMBER, NUMBER AND NUMBER. SO IT WILL FEEL ONLY GOOD COMFORTABLE FEELINGS.

(Slowly start to pinch the fleshy part of their skin between the base of their thumb and index finger with <u>your finger nails</u> of your thumb and index finger till you are pinching it hard. Don't let go. Now as you are still pinching raise their hand up to their eyes with your other hand and say,)

NOW OPEN YOUR EYES AND YOU WILL SEE HOW HARD I PINCHED YOU WITH MY FINGER NAILS. YOUR HAND IS IN A STATE OF ANESTHESIA SO IT DIDN'T FEEL ANY DISCOMFORT. NOW YOU SEE YOU ARE IN A STATE OF HYPNOSIS OR THIS WOULD HAVE HURT. (let go now of the pinch so they can see).

I WANT YOU TO BE AWARE OF HOW PERFECT YOUR BODY IS WORKING NOW. EACH AND EVERY CELL, MOLECULE, AND ATOM IS FUNCTIONING PERFECTLY AS GOD

INTENDED. EVERY ORGAN EVERY GLAND IS HEALTHY AND PERFECT. ALL YOUR VEINS AND ARTERIES ARE CLEAR AND HEALTHY. YOUR RED AND WHITE CORPUSCLES AND YOUR IMMUNE SYSTEM IS WORKING PERFECTLY. YOU FEEL GOOD, YOU FEEL FINE, YOU FEEL WONDERFUL IN EVERY WAY JUST AS GOD INTENDED. YOU FEEL CALM AND RELAXED THROUGHOUT YOUR ENTIRE BODY AND YOUR MIND IS CLEAR.

WHEN YOU OPEN YOUR EYES ON THE COUNT OF 5 YOU WILL TAKE THIS RELAXED AND WONDERFUL FEELING WITH YOU THE ENTIRE DAY. WHEN YOU DECIDE TO GO TO SLEEP TONIGHT AND YOU GET INTO BED YOU WILL INSTANTLY EMPTY YOUR MIND AND GO INTO A DEEP AND WONDERFUL RELAXED SLEEP. WITH HAPPY AND CONTENTED DREAMS GOING THROUGH YOUR MIND. SHOULD ANYTHING REQUIRE YOUR ATTENTION DURING THE NIGHT, YOU WILL BE INSTANTLY AWAKE AND TAKE CARE OF IT. THE MOMENT YOU GO BACK TO BED YOU AGAIN WILL BE ABLE TO GO INTO A WONDERFUL DEEP RESTFUL SLEEP WITH HAPPY AND CONTENTED DREAMS GOING THROUGH YOUR MIND.

WHEN YOU AWAKEN AT YOUR APPOINTED TIME, … YOU WILL BE SO REFRESHED AND WIDE-AWAKE, … FULL OF ENERGY….FROM SUCH A WONDERFUL NIGHT SLEEP….LOOKING FORWARD TO WHAT THE DAY HAS IN STORE FOR YOU.

DO NOT OPEN YOUR EYES TILL AFTER I COUNT 5. *(COUNT VERY SLOWLY).*

ONE,…..COMING UP MORE AND MORE……TWO FEELING MORE REFRESHED….. THREE ENERGY FLOWING BACK INTO YOUR BODY…..FOUR WIDER AWAKE….. AND ON THE COUNT OF FIVE TAKE PLENTY OF TIME BEFORE OPENING YOUR EYES FEELING FULLY REFRESHED AND AWAKE…..FIVE.

HOW TO TEST FOR SOMNAMBULISM

When they only twitch when you ask them to _try_ to lift their arms and legs and they can't open their eyes when you ask them to _try_ they are in Somnambulism and ready to be programmed for only good comfortable feelings if you want them to be pain free for any reason.

OUTLINE FOR SOMNAMBULISM

Do short induction to get eye closure.

Have them open and close their eyes 3 times (not until you tell them to).

Have them count backwards from 100 to 97, and loose numbers.

Ask them to try to move their right arm. Do the same for left arm, right leg, left leg. Then say, "Try to open eyes."

(the instant you see a twitch say, "OK stop trying)

If they only twitched limbs and couldn't open eyes, they're ready.

They are very deep at this point and ready for therapy. With suggestions for comfort they will also be anesthetized.

ESDAILE COMA STATE SCRIPT

(To achieve the Esdaile Coma state the somnambulism script is said first and then add this script. You must know how to test the patient to be sure they are in the Esdale Coma state. Never assume they are just because you said the script.)

I'D LIKE YOU TO TAKE A NICE LONG DEEP BREATH IN THROUGH YOUR NOSE AND LET IT OUT THROUGH YOUR MOUTH. GOOD. NOW TAKE ANOTHER NICE LONG DEEP BREATH IN THROUGH YOUR NOSE AND LET IT ALSO OUT THROUGH YOUR MOUTH, EXCELLENT. NOW TAKE A VERY LONG DEEP BREATH AND HOLD IT……… NOW LET IT OUT THROUGH YOUR MOUTH. YOU CAN FEEL YOURSELF GETTING MORE AND MORE RELAXED. WITH EVERY BREATH YOU EXHALE YOU CONTINUE TO GO DEEPER AND DEEPER RELAXED. DEEPER AND DEEPER RELAXED. ANY SOUNDS YOU HEAR IN THIS ROOM OR OUTSIDE OF THIS ROOM JUST REASSURES YOU EVERYTHING IS NORMAL. AND, THEREFORE, YOU FIND EVERY SOUND JUST GUIDES YOU DEEPER AND DEEPER RELAXED.

IN A MOMENT I AM GOING TO ASK YOU TO OPEN AND CLOSE YOUR EYES. WHEN I DO THIS YOU ARE GOING TO BE ABLE TO RELAX TWICE AS MUCH AS YOU ARE NOW. OPEN YOUR EYES AND CLOSE YOUR EYES. VERY GOOD. (REPEAT TWO MORE TIMES) RELAX AND LET YOURSELF BE COVERED WITH A BEAUTIFUL BLANKET OF RELAXATION ALL THE WAY DOWN TO YOUR TOES.

YOU WILL GO DEEPLY RELAXED BUT YOU WILL NOT GO TO SLEEP. (repeat)

(compliment them how good they are doing).

NOW PHYSICALLY YOU HAVE ALL THE RELAXATION WE NEED. WE WANT YOUR MIND TO BE JUST AS RELAXED AS YOUR BODY IS, SO I WANT YOU TO START COUNTING WHEN I TELL YOU TO…NOT BEFORE, FROM 100 TO 97. YOU CAN COUNT SILENTLY OR OUT LOUD WHICHEVER YOU PREFER. AS YOU COUNT YOU WILL GO TWICE AS RELAXED AS THE NUMBER BEFORE. NOW THE INTERESTING THING THAT WILL HAPPEN IS AS YOU INCREASE YOUR RELAXATION….THOSE NUMBERS JUST RELAX RIGHT OUT OF YOUR MIND. WANT IT TO HAPPEN AND JUST LET IT HAPPEN. ONLY YOU CAN MAKE IT HAPPEN. YOU CAN COUNT OUT LOUD OR SILENTLY. WHATEVER MAKES YOU FEEL COMFORTABLE.

NOW START COUNTING SLOWLY. *(DON'T YOU COUNT, THE CLIENT DOES THE COUNTING* (they will say 100) DEEPER AND DEEPER RELAXED AND START LETTING GO OF THE NUMBERS. (they will say 99) GOING DEEPER AND DEEPER….. LET THE NUMBERS DISAPPEAR OUT OF YOUR MIND….JUST AS THOUGH YOU ARE TURNING OFF A SWITCH IN YOUR MIND. (they will say 98*)* DOUBLE YOUR

RELAXATION AGAIN AND WATCH THE NUMBERS DISAPPEAR…..(they will say 97) (pause)

IF YOU FEEL THAT THERE ARE ANY MORE NUMBERS THERE, THEN IMAGINE ERASING THEM ALL OFF AT ONE TIME. NOD WHEN YOU FEEL THEY ARE ALL GONE.

(when they nod continue.)

NOW WE ARE GOING TO EXPERIENCE EVEN MORE RELAXATION ALL THE WAY TO THE BOTTOM OF RELAXATION. WE WILL BE GOING TO LEVEL A, LEVEL B, AND

LEVEL C, YOU CAN IMAGINE GOING DOWN ANY WAY YOU LIKE, DOWN AN ELEVATOR, AN ESCALATOR, A STAIRWAY, A SLIDE, OR GENTLY FLOATING ON A FEATHER OR CLOUD. YOU CAN GO IN ANY DIRECTION YOU LIKE OR NO PARTICULAR DIRECTION AT ALL, SUCH AS WHEN YOU ARE FLOATING. NOW WHEN I TELL YOU TO…NOT BEFORE, YOU WILL START GOING TO LEVEL "A", WHEN YOU REACH LEVEL "A" YOU WILL BE 10 TIMES MORE RELAXED THAN NOW. WHEN YOU REACH LEVEL "A" YOU WILL TRY TO SAY "A". START GOING NOW. (wait 10 seconds) OK STOP TRYING.

NOW WHEN I TELL YOU TO NOT BEFORE…YOU WILL START GOING TO LEVEL "B", WHEN YOU REACH LEVEL "B" YOU WILL BE 50 TIMES MORE RELAXED THAN NOW…AND WHEN YOU F I N A L Y REACH LEVEL "B" YOU WILL TRY TO SAY "B". START GOING NOW. (wait to 15 seconds) OK STOP TRYING.

THIS TIME WHEN I TELL YOU TO NOT BEFORE….YOU WILL GO TO LEVEL "C", AND WHEN YOU REACH LEVEL "C" YOU WILL BE 100 TIMES MORE RELAXED THAN NOW. AND WHEN YOU REACH LEVEL "C" YOU WILL TRY TO SAY "C". START GOING NOW. (wait 10 seconds) OK STOP TRYING.

(test then for how deep they are) TRY TO MOVE YOUR LEFT ARM, (as soon as they twitch say) GOOD STOP TRYING. NOW TRY TO MOVE YOUR RIGHT ARM, GOOD STOP TRYING. TRY TO MOVE YOUR LEFT LEG, FINE STOP TRYING. TRY TO MOVE YOUR RIGHT LEG, GOOD STOP TRYING. TRY TO OPEN YOUR EYES, OK STOP TRYING. YOU FEEL NO DISCOMFORT IN YOUR BODY…. ONLY GOOD COMFORTABLE FEELINGS THE DEEPER YOU GO. YOU ACCEPT ONLY GOOD SUGGESTIONS THAT SERVE YOUR BEST INTEREST. THOSE WILL GO INTO THE DEEPEST PART OF YOUR SUBCONSCIOUS AND UNCONSCIOUS MIND, AND YOU WILL BE SERVED BY THEM.

I WANT YOU TO BE AWARE OF HOW PERFECT YOUR BODY IS WORKING NOW. EACH AND EVERY CELL, MOLECULE, AND ATOM IS FUNCTIONING PERFECTLY AS GOD INTENDED. EVERY ORGAN EVERY GLAND IS HEALTHY AND PERFECT.

ALL YOUR VEINS AND ARTERIES ARE CLEAR AND HEALTHY. YOUR RED AND WHITE CORPUSCLES AND YOUR IMMUNE SYSTEM IS WORKING PERFECTLY. YOU FEEL GOOD, YOU FEEL FINE, YOU FEEL WONDERFUL IN EVERY WAY JUST AS GOD INTENDED. YOU FEEL CALM AND RELAXED THROUGHOUT YOUR ENTIRE BODY AND YOUR MIND IS CLEAR.

WHEN YOU OPEN YOUR EYES ON THE COUNT OF 5 YOU WILL TAKE THIS RELAXED AND WONDERFUL FEELING WITH YOU THE ENTIRE DAY. WHEN YOU DECIDE TO GO TO SLEEP TONIGHT AND YOU CRAWL INTO BED YOU WILL INSTANTLY EMPTY YOUR MIND AND GO INTO A DEEP AND WONDERFUL RELAXED SLEEP. WITH HAPPY AND CONTENTED DREAMS GOING THROUGH YOUR MIND. SHOULD ANYTHING REQUIRE YOUR ATTENTION DURING THE NIGHT, YOU WILL BE INSTANTLY AWAKE AND TAKE CARE OF IT. THE MOMENT YOU GO BACK TO BED YOU AGAIN WILL BE ABLE TO GO INTO A WONDERFUL DEEP RESTFUL SLEEP WITH HAPPY AND CONTENTED DREAMS GOING THROUGH YOUR MIND.

WHEN YOU AWAKEN IN THE MORNING AT YOUR APPOINTED TIME, … YOU WILL BE SO REFRESHED AND WIDE-AWAKE, … FULL OF ENERGY….FROM SUCH A WONDERFUL NIGHT SLEEP….LOOKING FORWARD TO WHAT THE DAY HAS IN STORE FOR YOU.

NOW WHEN I COUNT FROM ONE TO TEN YOU COME UP MORE AND MORE TO ALERTNESS. YOU WILL FEEL FULLY ALERT AND REFRESHED WHEN YOU OPEN YOUR EYES ON THE COUNT OF FIVE.

<u>DO NOT</u> OPEN YOUR EYES TILL AFTER I COUNT 10. (count very slowly).

ONE,…..COMING UP MORE AND MORE……TWO FEELING MORE REFRESHED….. THREE ENERGY FLOWING BACK INTO YOUR WIDER AWAKE….FOUR…..FIVE….. SIX…..SEVEN…..EIGHT…..NINE…..AND ON THE COUNT OF TEN TAKE PLENTY OF TIME BE TEN.

(When they open their eyes say,)
HOW DO YOU FEEL?

HOW TO TEST FOR THE ESDAILE COMA STATE

When you have the subject try to move each limb they will barely move them. They will move slightly the upper muscles in the legs.

When you ask them to try to open their eyes there will be no movement whatsoever of the eye muscles. Be sure not to say open your eyes because then it no longer is a test to see if they are able to or not.

If you see any eye movement at all take them down levels A, B, and C again to achieve the Coma State. Only on one occasion has a client of mine made eye movement and yet tested out to be in the Esdaile Coma State.

If there is no eye movement whatsoever then they are ready for the next test. Test them now for catatonia by stretching out their arms and legs one at a time. Do not say anything to indicate you want their arms to remain outstretched. If their limbs remain outstretched they are in the Esdaile Coma State. You can then lower each limb.

This is a good state for operations were they would be in an awkward position for any length of time. In this state they are still aware of their surroundings but will not respond to any command to move, etc.

When the subject is in the Esdaile Coma State they do not have to be told that they will not feel pain or discomfort as you must do when the subject is only in Somnambulism.

Since the subject is in a wonderful state of euphoria in the coma state they most likely will not emerge when you want them to with the usual procedure. To get them to emerge you must say the following; "If you ever wish to be in this wonderful state of hypnosis again you will open your eyes and be fully awake on the count of five." Count slower than usual since they are at a greater depth of hypnosis. This is the only way you will be able to emerge them.

OUTLINE FOR ESDAILE COMA STATE

Do short induction to get eye closure.

Have them open and close their eyes 3 times (not until you tell them to).

Have them count backwards from 100 to 97, and loose numbers.

Take them down level A, B, and C.

Ask them to try to move each limb. (the instant you see a twitch say, "OK stop trying).

Ask them to try to open eyes (If they only twitched limbs and do not twitch eyes they're in Esdaile Coma State.) They are very deep at this point and ready for therapy.

They are automatically anesthetized without you having to say anything.

DIFFERENCE BETWEEN ESDAILE COMA STATE AND SOMNAMBULISM

1. In Somnambulism you have to say they will feel no pain. In the Esdaile state it happens automatically.

2. In Somnambulism they will move etc. if you tell them to. In the Esdaile they are euphoric and will ignore you

3. Catatonic in the Esdaile State

4. You can count client out of Somnambulism. You have to tell client in the Esdaile State, "If you ever want to be this relaxed again you will open your eyes on the count of five and be fully awake and alert.

EMERGING AND GOOD AFFIRMATIONS

(Affirmation for someone that had dysfunctional upbringing)

THE REASONS FOR YOUR HAVING HAD THIS PROBLEM OF _____
ARE IN THE PAST AND IT IS OVER WITH. IT NO LONGER EXISTS AT THIS TIME
FOR YOU. IT IS OVER WITH, GONE FOREVER, NEVER TO HAPPEN AGAIN OR TO
BOTHER YOU. YOU ARE GROWN NOW. YOU ARE AN ADULT NOW, THEREFORE
YOU ARE IN CONTROL OF WHAT HAPPENS IN YOUR LIFE. IT IS IN THE PAST
LONG OVER WITH. IT CANNOT DISTURB YOU OR BOTHER YOU ANYMORE.
YOU WILL NOT ALLOW SOMETHING TO HAPPEN TO YOU AGAIN, BECAUSE
YOU ARE THE ADULT NOW AND CAN MAKE DECISIONS OF WHAT YOU WANT
IN YOUR LIFE. YOU AS AN ADULT DO NOT HAVE TO FEEL OUT OF CONTROL
AND HELPLESS AS YOU DID WHEN YOU WERE A SMALL CHILD. YOU ARE NOW
AN ADULT AND IN CONTROL AND IN CHARGE OF WHAT HAPPENS TO YOU.

NEGATIVE THOUGHTS AND SUGGESTIONS WILL HAVE NO INFLUENCE OVER
YOU. EVERY DAY IN EVERY WAY YOU ARE GETTING BETTER AND BETTER, AT
ANY MIND LEVEL. YOU WILL TOTALLY REJECT ANY NEGATIVE THOUGHTS
OR SUGGESTIONS. YOU WILL ACCEPT ONLY POSITIVE SUGGESTIONS AND
THOUGHTS. THIS SUGGESTION WILL BE ACCEPTED BY THE DEEPEST PART OF
YOUR SUBCONSCIOUS AND UNCONSCIOUS MIND, AND YOU WILL REACT TO
IT SINCE IT IS IN YOUR BEST INTEREST.

I WANT YOU TO BE AWARE OF HOW PERFECT YOUR BODY IS WORKING NOW.
EACH AND EVERY CELL, MOLECULE, AND ATOM IS FUNCTIONING PERFECTLY
AS GOD

INTENDED. EVERY ORGAN EVERY GLAND IS HEALTHY AND PERFECT. ALL
YOUR VEINS AND ARTERIES ARE CLEAR AND HEALTHY. YOUR RED AND WHITE
CORPUSCLES AND YOUR IMMUNE SYSTEM IS WORKING PERFECTLY. YOU FEEL
GOOD, YOU FEEL FINE, YOU FEEL WONDERFUL IN EVERY WAY JUST AS GOD
INTENDED. YOU FEEL CALM AND RELAXED THROUGHOUT YOUR ENTIRE
BODY AND YOUR MIND IS CLEAR.

WHEN YOU OPEN YOUR EYES ON THE COUNT OF 5 YOU WILL TAKE THIS RELAXED
AND WONDERFUL FEELING WITH YOU THE ENTIRE DAY. WHEN YOU DECIDE
TO GO TO SLEEP TONIGHT AND YOU GET INTO BED YOU WILL INSTANTLY
EMPTY YOUR MIND AND GO INTO A DEEP AND WONDERFUL RELAXED SLEEP.
WITH HAPPY AND CONTENTED DREAMS GOING THROUGH YOUR MIND.
SHOULD ANYTHING REQUIRE YOUR ATTENTION DURING THE NIGHT, YOU
WILL BE INSTANTLY AWAKE AND TAKE CARE OF IT. THE MOMENT YOU GO BACK

TO BED YOU AGAIN WILL BE ABLE TO GO INTO A WONDERFUL DEEP RESTFUL SLEEP WITH HAPPY AND CONTENTED DREAMS GOING THROUGH YOUR MIND.

WHEN YOU AWAKEN AT YOUR APPOINTED TIME, … YOU WILL BE SO REFRESHED AND WIDE-AWAKE, … FULL OF ENERGY….FROM SUCH A WONDERFUL NIGHT SLEEP….LOOKING FORWARD TO WHAT THE DAY HAS IN STORE FOR YOU.

DO NOT OPEN YOUR EYES TILL AFTER I COUNT 5. *(COUNT VERY SLOWLY)*.

IN A MOMENT I WILL COUNT FROM 1 TO 10. AT THE COUNT OF FIVE AND NOT BEFORE, YOU WILL OPEN YOUR EYES AND EMERGE FROM THIS VERY PLEASANT STATE OF RELAXATION. WHEN YOU EMERGE, YOU WILL FEEL WONDERFULLY RELAXED AND REFRESHED FULLY ALERT AS THOUGH YOU'VE HAD A NICE LONG NAP. YOU WILL REMEMBER EVERYTHING SAID WHILE YOU WERE IN THIS RELAXED STATE, AND YOU WILL ACCEPT ONLY SUGGESTIONS THAT WOULD BE TO YOUR BEST INTEREST. IF THERE WERE ANY TENSIONS FROM THE DAY'S ACTIVITIES THEY WILL DIMINISH AND DISAPPEAR. YOU WILL FEEL GREAT. WAIT TILL THE COUNT OF 5 TO SLOWLY OPEN YOUR EYES WHEN YOU FEEL READY.

1….2….3….4….5....6....7....8....9....10 EYES OPEN, FULLY ALERT, REFRESHED AND FEELING GREAT AND WONDERFUL IN EVERY WAY!

ALTERNATIVE TO HYPNOSIS

At times when hypnosis isn't necessay you can get yes and no answers from their subconscious mind by using Kinesiology (muscle testing).

I always explain what Muscle Testing is and then demonstrate it on the client as follows:

"ARE YOU FAMILIAR AND KNOW WHAT KINESIOLOGY OR MUSCLE TESTING IS? SOME CHIROPRACTORS AND HERBOLIGISTS USE IT.

LET ME DEMONSTRATE IT. HOLD YOUR ARM THAT IS CLOSEST TO ME UP TO YOUR SIDE.

WHEN I SAY RESIST AND PUSH GENTLY WITH MY TWO FINGERS ON YOUR WRIST YOU WANT TO KEEP YOUR ARM UP AT THE SAME LEVEL.

FIRST I'M GOING TO SEE IF YOU ARE IN BALANCE. LOOK STRAIGHT AHEAD. WITHOUT MOVING YOUR HEAD MOVE YOUR EYES TO THE LEFT. <u>RESIST</u> NOW MOVE YOUR EYES TO THE RIGHT <u>RESITS.</u>" (If their arm goes weak that is a sign that they are out of balance. Then you tell them to say six times,) I'M A WONDERFUL CHILD OF GOD AND NOTHING CAN HARM ME."

Test them again. Repeat if they still show a weakness.

Now you show them how it works.

"I'M GOING TO ASK YOU NOW TWO QUESTIONS THAT YOU KNOW THE ANSWER TO, BUT I DON'T WANT YOU TO SAY ANYTHING OUT LOUD.

IS YOU FIRST NAME <u>say their first name</u> RESIST" (Their arm should be strong.) IS YOU LAST NAME <u>give a wrong name</u> RESIST." (Their arm should be weak and go down some.)

"YOU SEE HOW IT WORKS. IF YOUR SUBCONSCIOUS MIND KNOWS WHAT THE CORRECT ANSWER IS EVEN IF YOUR CONSCIOUS MIND DOESN'T, IT WILL GIVE THE CORRECT SIGNAL LIKE THAT."

This can be used in or out of hypnosis. You will have occasions when this technique will be usefull.

BEST PROCEDURE IN HANDLING A BURN PATIENT

1. Try to see them within the first or second hours for best healing.

2. Do induction as quickly as possible and reduce pain first. This will give you credibility with them and they will be able to focus better on your healing suggestions.

3. Give them suggestions that the burn incident is over and done. So now their body can quit reacting to the burn and start sending healing to that area. Keep repeating these suggestions. Try to work on them for an hour.

Burn patients who normally would have had a moon face and their eyes swollen shut will not have that happen if they are worked on within two hours after the burn. They will heal in a fraction of the time it would have usually taken.

Give suggestions that it is not necessary for their body to react to the burn and the fluids in their body will not go to the burn area because they are healing, etc.

Give any other appropriate suggestions for comfort and fast healing.

SCRIPT FOR PROGRESSIVE HYPNOSIS AND POST HYPNOTIC SUGGESTIONS FOR GOOD HEALTH AND COMFORT

SET BACK, RELAX, NOW JUST CLOSE YOUR EYES. FOR IN A VERY FEW MOMENTS YOUR GOING TO BE MORE RELAXED THAN YOU HAVE EVER KNOWN YOURSELF TO BE BEFORE. IN ORDER TO HELP YOU TO RELAX I AM GOING TO MENTION CERTAIN PARTS OF YOUR BODY AND AS I DO _IN YOUR MIND AND IN YOUR IMAGINATION_ YOUR MIND WILL AUTOMATICALLY MAKE THAT PART OF YOUR BODY RELAX. MAKE THAT PART OF YOUR BODY BEGIN TO RELAX. I WOULD LIKE YOU TO MAKE THAT PART OF YOUR BODY BEGIN TO RELAX. MAKE THAT PART OF YOUR BODY BEGIN TO RELAX COMPLETELY.

I WANT YOU TO MAKE THAT PART OF YOUR BODY TO CONTINUE TO RELAX AS I MENTION EACH PART OF YOUR BODY.

CONCENTRATE ON YOUR FOREHEAD AND ALL THOSE FROWN LINES, ALL THE WORRY LINES, THEIR JUST BEGINNING TO DISAPPEAR AND THE FOREHEAD ITSELF STARTS TO SMOOTH OUT AND THAT RELAXATION IS TRAVELING DOWN AND AROUND THE CHEEKS AND ALL THE WAY OVER THE LIPS AND WITHIN THE MOUTH IS STAYING PERFECTLY MOIST AND COMFORTABLE.

THAT RELAXATION IS GOING OVER AND AROUND THE NECK AND OUT ALONG THE SHOULDERS AND IT FEELS AS IF THEIR'S A THOUSAND LITTLE FINGERS GENTLY MASSAGING EVERY MUSCLE AND EVERY NERVE ALONG THE SHOULDER AND ALL THE WAY DOWN THE SPINE.

THEN AROUND THE BUTTOCK AND DEEP WITHIN THE ORGANS THEMSELVES, DOWN THE LEGS AND OVER THE KNEES, AROUND THE CALVES, AROUND THE ANKLE AND INTO THE FEET THEMSELVES.

NOW TAKE A NICE GENTLE BREATH OF FRESH PURE ENERGY AND SLOWLY EXHALE AND RELEASE ALL THE TENSION OUT OF THE SPINE, VERTEBRA BY VERTEBRA. PUSH IT OUT, PUSH IT OUT.

ONCE AGAIN BREATHE EVER DEEPER SLOWLY ALLOWING THE ARMS TO DRIFT DOWN DEEPER AND DEEPER AND EVEN DEEPER RELAXED, CALM AND PEACEFUL. IN A WARM HEALING COLOR STARTING AT THE VERY TOP OF YOUR FOREHEAD SLOWLY FLOWING OVER YOUR ENTIRE BODY.

ALL THE WORRIES AND CONCERN ARE JUST FADING THAT YOUR THINKING AS A VERY PROFOUND AFFECT UPON YOUR HEALTH AND YOUR THOUGHTS CAN AND WILL AND DO AFFECT YOUR GENERAL WELL BEING AT ALL TIMES.

SO WHAT YOU HAVE PREVIOUSLY THOUGHT OF YOURSELF PERHAPS IS UNHEALTHY. YOUR NOW GOING TO REPLACE THOSE NEGATIVE THOUGHTS WITH POSITIVE ONES OF RADIANT HEALTHY, YOUTH, AND VIM, VIGOR, AND VITALITY. IMMENSELY ENJOYING ALL THAT YOUR LIFE HAS TO OFFER. YOUR REALIZING THAT ILLNESS CAN BE CAUSED BY YOUR LIFES DAY TO DAY STRESS AND STRAINS THAT APPLIES TO YOU.

YOUR GOING TO TACKLE THOSE AREAS WITHIN YOUR LIFE THAT COULD STAND SOME IMPROVEMENTS WITH CONFIDENCE, VITALITY AND RESOURCEFULNESS SENDING ALL THE PRINCIPLES OF PEACE AND RELAXATION THAT YOU ARE LEARNING RIGHT NOW. INTO THE AREAS OF YOUR LIFE TO BE A MORE CALM, HEALTHIER, RELAXED PERSON.

YOU DETERMINE NOW TO START BUILDING A LIFE STYLE THAT PROVIDES YOU WITH A NUTRITIONAL ATTENTION THAT YOUR BODY NEEDS AND YOUR SUBCONSCIOUS MIND IS NOW DIRECTED TO PRODUCE WHATEVER CHEMICALS NECESSARY TO HEAL YOUR ENTIRE BODY.

IF YOU ARE EXPERIENCING ANY PAIN THE MIND WILL SECRETE CHEMICALS TO LET THAT PAIN JUST FADE AWAY AND EACH AND EVERY DAY IN EVERY CONCEIVABLE WAY YOU ARE GROWING MORE RELAXED. FEELING YOUNGER, HEALTHIER AND HAVING MORE ENERGY AND FEELING BETTER THAN THE DAY BEFORE.

YOUR JOINTS ARE GOING TO BE FLEXIBLE AND COMFORTABLE AND YOUR IMMUNE SYSTEM, THOSE WHITE BLOOD CELLS ARE WORKING AS THEY SHOULD BE TO KEEP YOU FREE FROM ALL DISEASES. CIRCULATING WITHIN YOUR BLOOD STREAM.

CARING AWAY ALL THE DISEASE AND BACTERIA WITHIN YOUR BODY AND YOUR ARTERIES ARE SOFT, NORMAL AND PLIABLE AS FRESH OXYGEN REST AND CARRIES THE HEALING ELEMENTS TO THE UNIVERSE WITHIN YOUR BODY.

YOUR BLOOD PRESSURE WILL REMAIN NORMAL AS YOUR HEART BEATS STRONG AND RHYTHMICALLY. YOU NOW REALIZE THAT THE CREATOR OF THIS UNIVERSE HAS PRESENTED YOU WITH THE WORLDS MOST WONDERFUL MACHINE. HE HAS DESIGNED US TO BE ABLE TO HEAL ANYTHING, AND THAT YOUR OWN BODY AND THIS MIRACLE MACHINE HAS ITS OWN NON STOP MOTOR, YOUR HEART.

YOU'RE TAKING SPECIAL CARE OF THAT HEART. AVOID EATING FATTY FOODS. FATTY FOODS TASTE TOO GREASY FOR YOU. LEAN FOODS TASTE FRESH AND PURE TO YOU.

YOU ARE SLEEPING PROPERLY AND GETTING OUT AN EXERCISING A MINIMUM OF 10 MINUTES A DAY FOR THE FIRST WEEK, INCREASING FIVE MINUTES EACH WEEK UNTIL YOU ARE EXCERSIZING THIRTY MINUTES EACH AND EVERY DAY OR AS MUCH AS YOU CAN.

YOU HAVE YOUR OWN FEELING SYSTEM AND THAT IS THE DIGESTIVE TRACT. YOU BEGIN EVERY MEAL WITH A GLASS OF WATER WITHOUT ICE BEFORE YOU EAT YOUR MEAL. SINCE YOUR STOMACH IS NO LARGER THAN YOUR FIST YOU START WITH ONLY THAT AMOUNT ON YOUR PLATE. YOU ARE CHEWING YOUR FOOD SLOWER AND MORE RELAXED NOW, ALLOWING THE TEETH TO DO THEIR JOB. WHEN YOU EAT SLOWLY YOU ARE GIVING YOURSELVE THE PLESURE OF SAVORING EACH BITE.

IT FEELS GOOD AND EMPOWERING TO SAY NO THANK YOU, TO THE SECOND HELPINGS, THE FATTENING SWEETS, THE SALTS AND YOUR DIGESTIVE TRACT IS WORKING AS IT SHOULD BE. SIMULATING THE FOODS, THE VITAMINS AND MINERALS AND RELEASING THOSE ELEMENTS INTO YOUR BODY TO KEEP YOU HEALTHY AND HAPPY AND YOU HAVE
YOUR OWN NUTRITION SYSTEM AND THAT IS THE KIDNEYS AND YOUR DRINKING WONDERFUL FRESH CLEAR WATER. WATER IS THE BEVERAGE THAT IS SATISFYING YOU AND YOUR KIDNEYS ARE FLUSHING OUT ALL THE TOXINS, ALL THE DISEASE, ALL THE IMPURITIES WITHIN YOUR BODY AND ONCE IT HAS BEEN FLUSHED OUT IT WILL NEVER RETURN.

YOU HAVE YOUR OWN THINKING SYSTEM. THE BRAIN, AND YOUR TAKING IN LECTURES, LISTENING TO PROGRAMS AND READING MATERIAL TO HELP YOU KEEP AND REMAIN HEALTHY FOR EVER.

YOUR OWN TEMPERATURE CONTROL, YOUR SWEAT GLANDS ARE WORKING NORMALLY NOW. YOUR WORKING AND SLEEPING MORE COMFORTABLE EVERY DAY. YOUR TAKING EXTRA SPECIAL CARE OF YOUR BODY, GIVING IT EXTRA SPECIAL ATTENTION. YOU GIVE

YOUR GOING TO FOLLOW CERTAIN GUIDE LINES NOW. YOU RESOLVE TO DEVOTE PORTIONS OF TODAY TO IMPROVE YOUR HEALTH AND DEVOTE A PORTION OF YOUR DAY TO IMPROVE YOUR MIND. EXERCISING REGULARLY WHATEVER YOU ARE ABLE TO DO FOR 15 MINUTES A DAY FOR THE FIRST TWO WEEKS. YOU ADD FIVE MORE MINUTES EACH DAY WEEK THREE AND FOUR. YOU INCREASE THE TIME AS YOU FEEL YOU WANT TO AFTER THE FOURTH WEEK, GETTING OUT IN THE SUN.

ALLOWING YOUR BODY TO HAVE THE SLEEP AND EATING WHOLESOME GOOD FOOD AND NOT
OVER EATING OR DRINKING. YOU REALIZE NOW THAT AN OUNCE OF PREVENTION IS WORTH A POUND OF CURE. YOUR BODY IS GETTING WELL. TAKE A NICE DEEP BREATH NOW, IN THROUGH YOUR NOSE AND FILL YOUR LUNGS ALL THE WAY UP WITH AIR, NOW SLOWLY EXHALE THROUGH YOUR MOUTH. WHENEVER YOU WISH, REVIVE YOURSELF SLOWLY.

NOW TAKE YOUR TIME TO AROUSE YOURSELF, AND WHEN YOU FINALLY OPEN YOUR EYES YOU WILL FEEL VERY ALERT AND REFRESHED AS THOUGH YOU HAD A NICE TWO HOUR NAP.

STIMULATING YOUR IMMUNE SYSTEM

(You can read this to them or best to make a CD for them to listen to each day at home.

SIT BACK, RELAX, NOW JUST CLOSE YOUR EYES. FOR IN A VERY FEW MOMENTS YOUR GOING TO BE MORE RELAXED THAN YOU HAVE EVER KNOWN YOURSELF TO BE BEFORE. IN ORDER TO HELP YOU TO RELAX I AM GOING TO MENTION CERTAIN PARTS OF YOUR BODY AND AS I DO IN YOUR MIND AND IN YOUR IMAGINATION I WANT YOU TO MAKE THAT PART OF YOUR BODY BEGIN TO RELAX. I WANT YOU TO MAKE THAT PART OF YOUR BODY BEGIN TO RELAX COMPLETELY.

I WANT YOU TO TAKE THAT PART OF YOUR BODY TO CONTINUE TO RELAX. CONCENTRATE ON YOUR FOREHEAD AND ALL THOSE FROWN LINES, ALL THE WORRY LINES, THEIR JUST BEGINNING TO DISAPPEAR AND THE FOREHEAD ITSELF STARTS TO S M O O T H OUT AND THAT RELAXATION IS TRAVELING DOWN AND AROUND THE CHEEKS AND ALL THE WAY OVER THE LIPS AND WITHIN THE MOUTH IS STAYING PERFECTLY MOIST AND COMFORTABLE AND THAT RELAXATION IS GOING OVER AND AROUND THE NECK AND OUT ALONG THE SHOULDERS AND IT FEELS AS IF THEIR'S A THOUSAND LITTLE FINGERS GENTLY MASSAGING EVERY MUSCLE AND EVERY NERVE ALONG THE SHOULDER AND ALL THE WAY DOWN THE SPINE, AROUND THE BUTTOCK AND DEEP WITHIN THE ORGANS THEMSELVES, DOWN THE LEGS AND OVER THE KNEES, AROUND THE CALVES, AROUND THE ANKLE AND INTO THE FEET THEMSELVES.

NOW TAKE A NICE GENTLE BREATH OF FRESH PURE ENERGY AND SLOWLY EXHALE AND RELEASE ALL THE TENSION OUT OF THE SPINE, VERTEBRA BY VERTEBRA. PUSH IT OUT, PUSH IT OUT. ONCE AGAIN BREATHE EVER DEEPER SLOWLY ALLOWING THE ARMS TO DRIFT DOWN DEEPER AND DEEPER AND EVEN DEEPER RELAXED, CALM AND PEACEFUL. IN A WARM HEALING COLOR STARTING AT THE VERY TOP OF YOUR FOREHEAD SLOWLY CLOSE YOUR ENTIRE BODY AND ALL THE WORRIES AND CONCERN ARE JUST FADING.

YOUR THINKING AS A VERY PROFOUND AFFECT UPON YOUR HEALTH AND YOUR THOUGHTS CAN AND WILL AND DO AFFECT YOUR GENERAL WELL BEING AT ALL TIMES. SO WHAT YOU HAVE PREVIOUSLY THOUGHT OF YOURSELF PERHAPS IS UNHEALTHY. YOUR NOW GOING TO REPLACE THOSE NEGATIVE THOUGHTS WITH POSITIVE ONES OF RADIANT HEALTHY YOUTH AND VIM, VIGOR AND VITALITY. YOU IMMENSELY ENJOY ALL THAT YOUR LIFE HAS TO OFFER.

YOU'R REALIZING THAT ILLNESS CAN BE CAUSED BY YOUR LIFES DAY TO DAY STRESS AND STRAINS THAT APPLIES TO YOU. AND YOUR GOING TO TACKLE

THOSE AREAS WITHIN YOUR LIFE THAT COULD STAND SOME IMPROVEMENTS WITH CONFIDENCE, VITALITY AND RESOURCEFULNESS. YOU ARE SENDING ALL THE PRINCIPLES OF PEACE AND RELAXATION THAT YOU ARE LEARNING RIGHT NOW. INTO THE AREAS OF YOUR LIFE TO BE A MORE CALM, HEALTHIER, RELAXED PERSON AND YOU DETERMINE NOW TO START BUILDING A LIFE STYLE THAT PROVIDES YOU WITH A NUTRITIONAL ATTENTION THAT YOUR BODY NEEDS.

YOUR SUBCONSCIOUS MIND IS NOW DIRECTED TO PRODUCE WHATEVER CHEMICALS NECESSARY TO HEAL YOUR ENTIRE BODY AND IF YOU ARE EXPERIENCING ANY PAIN THE MIND WILL SECRETE CHEMICALS TO LET THAT PAIN JUST FADE AWAY AND EACH AND EVERY DAY IN EVERY CONCEIVABLE WAY YOU ARE GROWING MORE RELAXED. FEELING YOUNGER, HEALTHIER AND HAVING MORE ENERGY AND FEELING BETTER THAN THE DAY BEFORE.

WHY YOUR JOINTS ARE GOING TO BE FLEXIBLE AND COMFORTABLE AND YOUR IMMUNE SYSTEM, THOSE WHITE BLOOD CELLS ARE WORKING AS THEY SHOULD BE TO KEEP YOU FREE FROM ALL DISEASES. CIRCULATING WITHIN YOUR BLOOD STREAM. CARING AWAY ALL THE DISEASE AND BACTERIA WITHIN YOUR BODY AND YOUR ARTERIES ARE SOFT, NORMAL AND PLIABLE AS FRESH OXYGEN REST AND CARRIES THE HEALING ELEMENTS TO THE UNIVERSE WITHIN YOUR BODY. YOUR BLOOD PRESSURE WILL REMAIN NORMAL AS YOUR HEART BEATS STRONG AND RHYTHMICALLY.

YOU NOW REALIZE THAT THE CREATOR OF THIS UNIVERSE HAS PRESENTED YOU WITH THE WORLDS MOST WONDERFUL MACHINE AND THAT IS YOUR OWN BODY. THIS MIRACLE MACHINE HAS ITS OWN NON STOP MOTOR, YOUR HEART. YOU'RE TAKING SPECIAL CARE OF THAT HEART. AVOID EATING FATTY FOODS. FATTY FOODS TASTE TOO GREASY FOR YOU. LEAN FOODS TASTE FRESH AND PURE TO YOU.

YOU ARE SLEEPING PROPERLY AND GETTING OUT AND EXERCISING PERHAPS JUST TAKING A BRISK WALK A MINIMUM OF 10 TO 15 MINUTES EACH AND EVERY DAY FOR THE FIRST WEEK. YOU CONTINUE TO ADD A FEW MINUTES EACH WEEK BECAUSE YOU ARE FEELING MORE ENERGY WITH EVERY WEEK YOU ARE DOING SOME EXCERSIZING.

YOU HAVE YOUR OWN FEELING SYSTEM AND THAT IS THE DIGESTIVE TRACT. YOUR CHEWING YOUR FOOD SLOWER AND MORE RELAXED NOW. YOU SLOW DOWN YOUR EATING SO YOU CAN ENJOY AND SAVOR YOUR FOOD MORE, ALLOWING THE TEETH TO DO THEIR JOB.

IT FEELS GOOD TO SAY NO THANK YOU, TO THE SECOND HELPINGS, THE FATTENING SWEETS, THE SALTS AND YOUR DIGESTIVE TRACT IS WORKING AS IT SHOULD BE, SIMULATING THE FOODS, THE VITAMINS AND MINERALS

AND RELEASING THOSE ELEMENTS INTO YOUR BODY TO KEEP YOU HEALTHY AND HAPPY AND YOU HAVE YOUR OWN NUTRITION SYSTEM AND THAT IS THE KIDNEYS. YOUR DRINKING WONDERFUL FRESH CLEAR WATER. WATER IS THE BEVERAGE THAT IS SATISFYING YOU AND YOUR KIDNEYS ARE FLUSHING OUT ALL THE TOXINS, ALL THE DISEASE, ALL THE IMPURITIES WITHIN YOUR BODY AND ONCE IT HAS BEEN FLUSHED OUT IT WILL NEVER RETURN. YOU HAVE YOUR OWN THINKING SYSTEM. THE BRAIN, AND YOUR TAKING IN LECTURES, LISTENING TO PROGRAMS AND READING MATERIAL TO HELP YOU KEEP AND REMAIN HEALTHY FOR EVER. YOUR OWN TEMPERATURE CONTROL,

YOUR SWEAT GLANDS ARE WORKING NORMALLY NOW. YOUR WORKING AND SLEEPING MORE COMFORTABLE EVERY DAY AND YOUR TAKING EXTRA SPECIAL CARE OF YOUR BODY, GIVING IT EXTRA SPECIAL ATTENTION. YOU GIVE ATTENTION TO YOURSELF PHYSICALLY AS WELL AS MENTALLY AND EMOTIONALLY. BECAUSE OF THIS YOUR GOING TO FOLLOW CERTAIN GUIDE LINES NOW. YOU RESOLVE TO DEVOTE PORTIONS OF TODAY TO IMPROVE YOUR HEALTH AND DEVOTE A PORTION OF YOUR DAY TO IMPROVE YOUR MIND. EXERCISING REGULARLY WHATEVER YOU ARE ABLE TO DO FOR AT LEAST 10 TO 15 MINUTES EACH DAY. GETTING OUT IN THE SUN EARLY MORNING OR LATER IN THE DAY.

ALLOWING YOUR BODY TO HAVE THE SLEEP AND EATING WHOLESOME GOOD FOOD. YOU EAT AND DRINKING SLOWLY TO ENJOY YOUR FOOD AND FIND THAT BY LISTENING TO YOUR BODY YOU EAT ONLY ENOUGH TO SATISFY YOURSELF AND NO MORE. YOU REALIZE YOUR STOMACH IS ABOUT THE SIZE OF YOUR FIST AND THAT AMOUNT OF FOOD SATISFIES YOU WHEN YOU EAT SLOWLY. YOUR BODY IS GETTING WELL.

TAKE A NICE DEEP BREATH NOW, IN THROUGH YOUR NOSE AND FILL YOUR LUNGS ALL THE WAY UP WITH CLEAN FRESH AIR. NOW SLOWLY EXHALE THROUGH YOUR MOUTH. WHENEVER YOU WISH, REVIVE YOURSELF SLOWLY. TAKE YOUR TIME TO AROUSE YOURSELF, AND WHEN YOU FINALLY OPEN YOUR EYES YOU WILL FEEL VERY ALERT AND REFRESHED AS THOUGH YOU HAD A NICE TWO HOUR NAP.

SOLID TUMORS

(The following imagery has had good results with solid tumors disappearing. A CD can be made of this for them to listen to each day as a re-enforcement.)

I WOULD LIKE YOU TO IMAGINE YOUR TUMOR WHAT THE SHAPE AND SIZE IS. NOW I WOULD LIKE YOU TO IMAGINE DROPPING IT IN A LARGE GLASS OF WATER AND IMAGINE WATCHING IT DISSOLVE LIKE AN ALKISELSER TABLET IN A GLASS OF WATER. KEEP IMAGINING WATCHING IT AS IT CONTINUES TO DISSOLVE LIKE AN ALKISELSER TABLET IN A GLASS OF WATER. WHEN IT IS ALL DISSOLVED NOD YOUR HEAD. NOW IMAGINE IT IS BEING FLUSHED OUT OF YOUR BODY AND ELIMINATED IN THE NORMAL WAY. NOD YOUR HEAD WHEN YOU ARE DONE AND WHEN IT IS ALL FLUSHED OUT OF YOUR BODY IN A NORMAL WAY.

(Instruct them to do this three times a day. It is not necessary for them to be in a state of self-hypnosis. They are already in that state as they are focused on those thoughts. Regression therapy would be advisable, especially if it is malignant.)

FATTY TUMORS OR GANGLION CYSTS

The above imagery does not work with a fatty tumor or ganglion cyst. This is probably due to the fact that fat wouldn't dissolve in water.

A friend of mine got rid of her ganglion cyst by tapping it whenever she thought about it during each day and saying,

I DON'T NEED THIS, I DON'T WANT THIS, AND I WANT THIS TO GO AWAY NOW. (Repeating this statement several times as she was tapping on it. She wasn't certain how long it took till it was gone. Perhaps about a month.)

(The above quote should also be added at the end of each imagery session for any tumors, illness, or any physical problem.)

IMAGINE WATCHING YOUR TUMOR/GANGLION CYST AS A HEAVY WET SPONGE. NOW START SQUEEZING THIS SPONGE. SQUEEZING OUT ALL THE HEAVY FLUID. AS YOU KEEP SQUEEZING THE SPONGE NOTICE IT IS SHRINKING... SHRINKING.....AND SHRINKING. JUST AS A SPONGE SHRINKS WHEN YOU SQUEEZE OUT ALL THE WATER. JUST IMAGINE HOW MUCH SMALLER A SPONGE IS WHEN IT IS SQUEEZED OUT AND DRY. WHEN YOU HAVE IT ALL SQUEEZED OUT AND DRY, NOD YOUR HEAD. OK, NOW I WOULD LIKE YOU TO IMAGINE IT GETTING EVEN DRYER. SO DRY IT IS GETTING BRITTLE AND STARTING TO CRUMBLE INTO DUST. WHEN IT IS ALL CRUMBLED INTO DUST YOUR BODY WILL FLUSH IT OUT AND ELIMINATE IT IN THE USUAL WAY FROM YOU BODY.

NOD YOUR HEAD WHEN THAT IS DONE."

REPEAT THE FOLLOWING AT LEAST 3 TIMES A DAY FOR RAPID HEALING

(Best If You Do It 5 Times A Day Or As Often As You Can)

I don't need this, I don't want this, I want it to go away now never to return.

I don't need this, I don't want this, I want it to go away now never to return.

I don't need this, I don't want this, I want it to go away now never to return.

I feel great, I feel good, I feel marvelous in every way. I have no discomfort in my body only good comfortable feelings though out my body.

I feel great, I feel good, I feel marvelous in every way. I have no discomfort in my body only good comfortable feelings though out my body.

I feel great, I feel good, I feel marvelous in every way. I have no discomfort in my body only good comfortable feelings though out my body.

I want my body to send all the healing to that part of my body now. I real rapidly and quickly.

I want my body to send all the healing to that part of my body now. I real rapidly and quickly.

I want my body to send all the healing to that part of my body now. I real rapidly and quickly.

(Now imagine it happening in your body.)

I did this when I had fractured my right elbow through all the horrible pain and tears. By the second morning when I woke up I had no pain and I was able to completely move my are and do anything that I had normally done. It amazed even me how fast it healed.

The Doctor had told me it would take six weeks. He had put my arm in a sling. The pain was incredible. I couldn't move it or straighten it out.

HEALING THROUGH IMAGERY

Always find out at the very beginning with a client if they are visual when their eyes are closed. The way to find out is ask them to close their eyes and **think** of a room at home and the objests in that room. Then ask them if they can picture and see everything or if they just remember everything. Most people are visual and can see when their eyes are closed. I myself do not. If you use visual terminalogy with some one who can't see anything with their eyes closed they will not be able to respond and will finally get frustrated and upset. Use only words like, imagin, remember, feel, recall. Never use visual words. I have trained myself never to use visual terminalogy because that way I din't slip up and people who can see with their eyes closed still can respond. If I do catch myself using a visual word I emediately also say the non-visual word.

When I had a small blood vessel break in my right eye I couldn't see in the center of my vision when I covered my left eye. I could see around the edges of my vision but not in the center. I was scheduled for laser surgery in thee months.

I pretended I had an eraser on the end of my index finger and I would point it towards my right eye about three inches from my eye and I pretended that I was erasing the blind spot. I did this as often as I would think about it for about one minute each day.

By the time the laser surgery came up I had vision in my right eye except that that center area was like looking through the wrong end of a telescope.

I then imagined I was placing my thumb, index finger, and middle finger in the center of my eye and spreading the opening wider. In a short period of time my sight was normal and has stayed normal for over ten years now.

PROGRAM YOURSELF FOR RAPID HEALING AND NO BLEEDING BEFORE YOU ARE GOING TO HAVE SURGERY

I have had two total knee replacement and two major back surgeries in the last 12 years. The last back surgery they straightened my scoliosis and but rods on each side of my back.

When I knew I was scheduled for surgery each time I would repeat dozens of time each day, "I do not bleed. I heal rapidly."

I'd repeat it many times every time I thought about it each day.

Ten days after each knee implant I was able to walk without a limp without a walker or cane and no pain.

The third day after my second back surgery after they had put in the rods I was walking the hospital halls without limping or a walker or cane. The nurse who would walk me around the halls couldn't belie it. I also did not feel any pain.

I must say that for the second surgery I insisted the Doctor use sutures and not staples which I found to be extremely painful for the first surgery until they where finally removed. It was like having nails drilled into my back.

I might also add that I hardly bled for any of these surgeries.

SCRIPT FOR PURGING PAST FEELINGS AND EMOTIONS THAT ARE CAUSING THE PHYSICAL PROBLEMS

(You can make a CD for them to listen to each day.)

SUBCONSCIOUS PURGING OF PAST NEGATIVE EMOTIONS
Igloo Script
(Good to use at the beginning of every session)

This is an excellent technique for purging the client's subconscious of generally negative thought and emotional energies from their past. This script is similar to Walter Sichort's, but reworded so you will get better results when working with clients that are not visual with their eyes closed.

Say the following to the client after you have done an induction:

REMAIN COMFORTABLE, AND RELAXED, GOING DEEPER RELAXED WITH EVERY BREATH THAT YOU TAKE. IMAGINE YOURSELF IN A COMFORTABLE, SMALL AND VERY PLEASANT WHITE WALLED ROOM, MUCH LIKE AN IGLOO. YOU DO NOT HAVE TO SEE IT; YOU CAN JUST IMAGINE IT. YOU ARE TOTALLY FREE OF ANY CLAUSTROPHOBIC FEELING…YOU JUST FEEL WELCOME, RIGHT AT HOME, HERE.

THIS ROOM IS A SMALL AND WHITE WALLED ROOM. YOU NOW SENSE THAT THIS WHITE WALLED ROOM IS ACTUALLY YOUR OWN SUBCONSCIOUS MIND… THE CORE OF YOUR BEING…THE VERY CENTER OF YOU.

YOU NOW NOTICE AND IMAGINE THAT CLINGING TO THE WALLS OF THIS ROOM…ALL OVER…ARE LITTLE BITS OF WHAT SEEM TO BE PAPER… IMAGINE SOME ARE RED AND SOME ARE WHITE. MOVING CLOSER TO THE WALL, YOU SENSE THAT STORED ON THE RED BITS OF WHAT SEEM TO BE PAPER, ARE ALL THE NEGATIVE THOUGHTS AND EMOTIONAL ENERGIES AND FEELINGS FROM ALL YOUR PAST. LIKE FEAR, DOUBT, GUILT, HATRED, ANXIETY, REJECTION, UNHAPPINESS!… ALL THE NEGATIVE, DEPRESSING, INHIBITING, DEFEATING, THOUGHT AND EMOTIONAL ENERGIES AND FEELINGS FROM YOUR PAST ARE STORED IN THIS ROOM OF YOUR SUBCONSCIOUS, ON THESE LITTLE RED BITS OF WHAT SEEM TO BE PAPER.

NOTICE THAT ON THE WHITE BITS OF WHAT SEEM TO BE PAPER, ARE ALL THE LOVELY, HAPPY, POSITIVE, AND UP LIFTING THOUGHTS AND EMOTIONAL ENERGIES AND FEELINGS. LIKE LOVE, PEACE, JOY, HAPPINESS, SELF-CONFIDENCE, SELF-ACCEPTANCE, FORGIVENESS OF SELF, AND OF OTHERS,

SUCCESS, AND CONTENTMENT... ALL OF THESE BEAUTIFUL, UP-LIFTING, POSITIVE, THOUGHT AND EMOTIONAL ENERGIES AND FEELINGS ARE STORED ON THESE WHITE BITS OF WHAT SEEM TO BE PAPER.

NOW BECOME AWARE OF THIS: YOU CAN PULL THESE RED BITS OF WHAT SEEM TO BE PAPER DOWN FROM THE WALL, YOU CAN CRUMPLE THEM IN YOUR HANDS UNTIL YOUR HANDS ARE FULL. YOU CAN TAKE THEM OVER TO WHERE A HOLE HAS OPENED IN THE CENTER OF THE FLOOR. DROP THEM THROUGH THAT HOLE. NOTICE THEM DISAPPEAR INTO NOTHINGNESS...SO THAT THESE CAN NEVER GET BACK IN AGAIN!

YOU CAN SENSE THAT, WITH A FEW TRIPS, GATHERING DOWN HANDFULS AND CARRYING THEM TO THE HOLE AND DROPPING THEM THROUGH, YOU CAN CLEAN ALL THE NEGATIVE THOUGHT AND EMOTIONAL ENERGIES FROM YOUR INNER SELF. NOW AT THE COUNT OF "ONE", I WANT YOU TO START WORKING AT IT.

I WILL SIT QUIETLY AND WAIT UNTIL YOU ARE FINISHED. WHEN YOU ARE THROUGH, JUST LET ME KNOW BY NODDING YOUR HEAD WHEN YOU ARE FINISHED. IF YOU ARE HAVING ANY DIFFICULTY GETTING ANY DOWN JUST LET ME KNOW VERBALLY THAT ONE IS STUCK.

NOW START AT THE COUNT OF "ONE" AND CLEAN IT UP. THREE...TWO...ONE.

(If they seem to be having a struggle or distress, ask, "What's going on?" If they say they can't get one down ask them "Which one is it that won't come down." They'll say hate, fear, etc. Then say, "All right, get hold of it. At the count of "one" both of us will pull it and it will fall off. Three... Two,...One!" (Snap finger, but not too loudly.)

(If they still can't get it down simply suggest that they remember this one and leave it for now and go on to the others, and to nod their head when they are done. Explain that they can deal with any they didn't get down because they can deal with those later, so they don't have to worry about it.) (When the client nods their head say,)

"THANK YOU...GOOD JOB!"

NOW NOTICE AND IMAGINE THAT THE WHITE BITS...THE GOOD, POSITIVE, ENERGIZING HELPFUL THOUGHTS AND EMOTIONAL ENERGIES AND FEELINGS ARE EXPANDING...GROWING TO FILL ALL THE SPACE LEFT BY THE RED ONES YOU DISPOSED OF...GROWING, EXPANDING!...UNTIL THEY FILL THE WHOLE WALLS AND CEILINGS WITH BEAUTIFUL, WONDERFUL, POSITIVE, WHITE. FEEL THE RESURGENCE OF POSITIVE ENERGY NOW WITHIN YOURSELF, AS YOU NOTICE AND IMAGINE THAT THE HOLE IN THE FLOOR HAS CLOSED ITSELF, AND THE ENTIRE ATMOSPHERE OF THE ROOM IS BECOMING WHITE... BEAUTIFUL, PURE, UPLIFTING, ENERGIZING WHITE. TAKE A DEEP BREATH AND

INHALE THE PURITY…THE STRENGTH THE SELF-CONFIDENCE… THE LOVE… THE PEACE… THE ASSURANCE… THE FREEDOM OF THIS ATMOSPHERE! FEEL IT, PERMEATING EVERY CELL AND EVERY ATOM OF YOUR BEING!

FROM THIS MOMENT FORWARD, MOMENT BY MOMENT, MINUTE BY MINUTE, HOUR BY HOUR, AND DAY BY DAY, THE THOUGHT AND EMOTIONAL ENERGIES OF YOUR SUBCONSCIOUS REMAIN SO POSITIVE, SO CALM, SO STABLE… LIKE NOW, THAT EVERY PART OF YOU… BODY AND MIND… REMAINS CALM, OBJECTIVE, CREATIVE. IT FUNCTIONS TO ABSOLUTE PERFECTION, JUST THE WAY GOD DESIGNED AND MADE YOU TO FUNCTION. (BRIEF PAUSE)

AT THE COUNT OF "ONE," THIS WILL ALL DISAPPEAR, BUT THE BEAUTIFUL, POSITIVE EFFECTS WILL CONTINUE. THREE… TWO… ONE!… IT DISAPPEARS AND YOU ARE BEAUTIFULLY RELAXED, RESTING BEAUTIFULLY… HERE IN MY OFFICE.

From here, you proceed either to some form of analysis or specific therapy, or simply issue the usual post-hypnotic, and pre-awakening suggestions, and emerge the client.

This exercise will be beneficial to every client. However, I suggest that direct subconscious questioning and/or regression is carried out to make sure that all that has caused their problem has been resolved. <u>Regression should only be done by a hypnotherapist who has had training to do this properly or it could cause trauma in the patient if done incorrectly.</u>

For best results this previous or next technique should be done for each session. That will remove particular emotions that is directly related to their problem. Repeated sessions will, usually, be successful in removal.

SUBCONSCIOUS KNOWS HOW TO LET GO

(Parts taken from Dr. Art Winklers script book.)

After doing the induction read this script to purge the subconscious from what has been causing the problem. Doing this one time may not be enough. You can do this at the beginning of a session or at the end.

YOUR SUBCONSCIOUS MIND CAN UIDERSTAND THINGS THAT YOU DO NOT CONSCIOUSLY UNDERSTAND, AND YOUR SUBCONSCIOUS MIND CAN WORK OUT SOLUTIONS TO PROBLEMS THAT YOU DON'T KNOW THE ANSWER TO...

I DON'T KNOW WHAT CAUSED YOU TO START HAVING THE PROBLEM OF_____ AND IT'S NOT NECESSARY FOR ME TO KNOW, NOR IS IT NECESSARY FOR YOU TO CONSCIOUSLY KNOW WHAT CAUSED YOU TO START...

WHAT EVER CAUSED YOU TO START HAVING THE PROBLEM OF_____
IS PAST NOW, AND YOUR SUBCONSCIOUS MIND IS UNDERSTANDING THAT THERE IS NO REASON IT NEEDS TO CONTINUE CAUSING YOU DIFFICULTY... YOUR SUBCONSCIOUS MIND CAN REVIEW THE IMPRINTS, IMPRESSIONS, THOUGHTS, IDEAS, AND MEMORIES IN YOUR MIND THAT HAVE CAUSED YOU TO CONTINUE HAVING THIS PROBLEM AND CAN ASSESS THAT INFORMATION AND REALIZE THERE IS NO REASON YOU NEED TO CONTINUE HAVING THIS PROBLEM.

WHEN YOUR SUBONSCIOUS MIND UNDERSTAND WHAT CAUSED YOU TO START HAVING THIS PROBLEM, AND REALIZES THERE IS NO REASON YOU NEED TO CONTINUE HAVING THE PROBLEM OF_____, YOUR SUBCONSIOUS MIND WILL CAUSE ONE OF THE FINGERS ON YOUR RIGHT HAND TO LIFT/ RIGHT UP TOMARDS THE CEILING, AND YOUR FINGER WILL REMAIN UP UNTIL I TELL IT TO GO BACK DOWN...

WHILE I'M WAITING FOR YOUR SUBCONSCIOUS MIND TO REVIEW WHAT HAS BEEN CAUSING YOU TO HAVE THIS PROBLEM, AND UNDERSTAND THE CAUSES AND EFFECTS, AND REALIZES THAT YOU CAN NOW BE FREE FROM HAVING THIS PROBLEM ANYMORE, I WILL SIT QUIETLY AND WAIT FOR ONE OF YOUR FINGERS TO SIGNAL.

They don't always signal the first time you do this. If they don't within about ten or fifteen minutes continue with the rest of the therapy or if you are doing this at the end of the session just tell them:

I WOULD LIKE ALL THE DIFFERENT PARTS OF YOUR MIND, YOUR INNER WISDOM, AND YOUR HIGHER SELF TO CONTINUE TO REVIEW AND RESOLVE WHATEVER WOULD STILL CAUSE THIS PROBLEM, UNTIL I SEE YOU AGAIN.

DOING IT IN A GENTLE WAY SO IT WILL NOT INTERFER WITH YOUR SLEEP AND WILL NOT DISTURB YOU DURING THE DAY. (Weather I do the above script of not I close with this statement after every session unless they had a very abusive childhood. Then I don't do this because after they leave their subconscious could cause trauma.

FREE FROM SMOKING SCRIPT

CLOSE YOUR EYES. INSIDE OF YOUR EYELIDS, JUST LOOK UP AS THOUGH YOU'RE TRYING TO LOOK AT YOUR EYEBROWS. YOU'LL NOTICE HOW TIRED IT MAKES YOUR EYES. HOW TIRED AND HOW DROWSY AND HEAVY IT MAKES YOUR EYES FEEL. YOU CAN RELAX YOUR EYES WHENEVER IT FEELS COMFORTABLE TO YOU.

I WILL COUNT FROM FIVE DOWN TO ONE AND AS I DO YOUR EYES GET MORE AND MORE TIRED. IF YOUR EYES AREN'T RELAXED AT THE COUNT OF ONE, THEN JUST ALLOW THEM TO RELAX. FIVE . . . HEAVIER AND HEAVIER, FOUR . . . MORE AND MORE TIRED, THREE . . . TWO . . . ONE . . . . NOW JUST RELAX YOUR EYES COMPLETELY AND TOTALLY AND SEND ALL THAT RELAXED FEELING THROUGH AND AROUND YOUR EYES, ALL THE WAY DOWN THROUGH YOUR BODY CLEAR TO THE VERY TIPS OF YOUR TOES.

I'D LIKE YOU TO TAKE A REAL LONG DEEP BREATH, IN THROUGH YOUR NOSE AND THEN EXHALE IT THROUGH YOUR MOUTH. JUST LETTING GO, GOING DEEPER RELAXED,—VERY GOOD ANOTHER REAL LONG DEEP BREATH, ALL THE WAY IN THROUGH YOUR NOSE AND EXHALE IT THROUGH YOUR MOUTH, GOING MORE DEEPLY RELAXED. NOW THE NEXT ONE ALL THE WAY IN AND HOLD IT. *(PAUSE)*

O.K. NOW LET IT ALL THE WAY OUT. YOU CAN FEEL HOW YOUR BODY IS JUST LETTING GO AND RELAXING NOW, GOING DEEPER AND DEEPER, RELAXED WITH EVERY BREATH THAT YOU EXHALE.

ANY SOUND THAT YOU MIGHT HEAR IN THIS ROOM OR OUTSIDE OF THIS ROOM JUST REASSURES YOU THAT EVERYTHING IS NORMAL. EVERY SOUND, THEREFORE, WILL GUIDE YOU DEEPER AND DEEPER RELAXED. DEEPER AND DEEPER RELAXED. THE MORE DEEPLY RELAXED YOU GO, THE BETTER YOU FEEL. DEEPER AND DEEPER RELAXED. DEEPER AND DEEPER RELAXED. *(PAUSE)*

NOW CONTINUING TO GO DEEPER RELAXED WITH EVERY BREATH THAT YOU EXHALE AND WITH EVERY SOUND THAT YOU HEAR GUIDING YOU DEEPER AND DEEPER RELAXED. YOU HAVE MADE THE DECISION THAT YOU NO LONGER WANT TO BE BURDENED AND TO BE A SLAVE OF CIGARETTES. THAT IS A GOOD AND WISE DECISION. YOU ALSO WANT TO BE FREE OF IT NOW.

YOU WANT TO BE FREE OF IT NOW—THIS INSTANT. BECAUSE YOU FEEL THIS WAY SO STRONGLY, YOU WILL FIND IT WILL BE EASY FOR YOU TO BE A NON-SMOKER. BECAUSE BY NATURE YOU ARE A NON-SMOKER. YOU WERE BORN A NON-SMOKER. BY THE MERE FACT THAT YOU WERE TO BREATHE AIR, YOU HAVE ALWAYS BEEN A NON-SMOKER.

YOU HAD TO ACTUALLY MAKE YOURSELF AND FORCE YOURSELF TO BREATHE SMOKE IN THE BEGINNING, BECAUSE BY NATURE THAT IS AN UNNATURAL THING TO DO. IT IS A DESTRUCTIVE, UNCOMFORTABLE AND UNNATURAL THING TO DO.

YOU HAVE MADE YOURSELF DO IT FOR SO LONG THAT YOU HAVE NOT REALIZED ANY MORE HOW TERRIBLE IT TASTES AND HOW TERRIBLE IT FEELS TO HAVE THE SMOKE THAT IS SEARING AND BURNING DOWN INTO YOUR LUNGS, GOING THROUGH

YOUR NOSE AND DOWN INTO YOUR THROAT INTO YOUR LUNGS. I'D LIKE YOU TO RECALL NOW; THE VERY FIRST TIME THAT YOU EVER TRIED TO INHALE. HOW HOT THAT SMOKE AND HOW BURNING IT WAS, AND HOW BAD IT TASTED. YOU MAY HAVE THOUGHT IT SMART TO DO THAT, BUT I WANT YOU TO RECALL NOW JUST HOW IT SMELLED, HOW IT TASTED. DO YOU RECALL? I WANT YOU TO INTENSIFY THAT TASTE AND BURNING FOR NOW, AS I COUNT FROM ONE TO FIVE THE TASTE AND BURNING IS GOING TO GET STRONGER, AND STRONGER. YOU WILL REMEMBER. YOU WILL POSSIBLY EVEN TASTE THE TASTE AGAIN.

ONE . . . GETTING STRONGER AND STRONGER. TWO . . .COMING UP, GETTING VERY INTENSE. THREE . . . VERY STRONG NOW. FOUR . . . EVEN MORE INTENSE. FIVE . . . COMPLETELY UP NOW. VERY INTENSE, VERY STRONG. THAT TASTE IS VERY STRONG—REMEMBER THAT TASTE AND BURNING. IT WAS VERY STRONG, VERY UNPLEASANT. WHEN YOU TOOK A DEEP BREATHE AND INHALED THE SMOKE THE FIRST TIME, DID YOU COUGH?

IT IS A VERY, VERY UNPLEASANT EXPERIENCE. YOU FEEL GROWN UP BUT IT DOES MAKE YOU FEEL PHYSICALLY BAD IT IS A VERY UNPLEASANT EXPERIENCE. THE TASTE IS AWFUL AND THE EXPERIENCE IS TRULY NOT A PLEASANT EXPERIENCE. IT IS A VERY UNPLEASANT EXPERIENCE. NOW THIS IS HOW CIGARETTES TASTE AND SMELL TO YOU FROM NOW ON. SO YOU HAVE NO INTENTION EVEN TO TRY TO SMOKE A CIGARETTE AGAIN, CIGARETTES STILL TASTE AND SMELL THE SAME BUT YOU GOT USED TO THE BAD TASTE AND SMELL IT HAS NICOTINE.

IT IS A STIMULANT AND KEYS YOU UP. BY NOT SMOKING ANY LONGER YOU WILL FIND YOU WILL BE MORE RELAXED AND CALMER BECAUSE YOU ARE ELIMINATING THE NICOTINE, WHICH IS A STIMULANT. AND THEREFORE YOU WILL BE RELAXED AT EASE AND MORE CALM.

YOU WILL BE SURPRISED HOW EASY IT IS FOR YOU TO BE VERY RELAXED AND FIND THAT BEING A NON-SMOKER IS A VERY PLEASURABLE, RELAXING CALMING EXPERIENCE. IF FOR SOME REASON YOU FEEL STRESS FOR WHATEVER REASON, YOU'LL FIND THAT ALL YOU NEED TO DO TO GET RID OF THAT FEELING AND OF THAT NEED, IS TO JUST SAY TO YOURSELF VERY CLEARLY IN YOUR

OWN MIND "NO I DON'T NEED THAT." AS YOU TAKE THREE DEEP BREATHS IN THROUGH YOUR NOSE AND EXHALE THROUGH YOUR MOUTH YOU WILL FIND THAT BY SAYING AND DOING THIS THREE TIMES. THE NEED FOR THE CIGARETTE WILL BE GONE. YOU WILL HAVE ABSOLUTELY NO NEED FOR A CIGARETTE YOU WILL FEEL IN CONTROL *(Repeat)*.

THIS SUGGESTION IS A VERY STRONG SUGGESTION. ALL YOU NEED TO DO IS TAKE THREE BREATHS AND SAY TO YOURSELF THE WORDS "NO I DON'T NEED THAT" THREE TIMES AND THE STRESS WILL BE LESS OR COMPLETELY GONE.

YOU WILL FEEL MORE RELAXED. THEREFORE THE NEED FOR A CIGARETTE WILL BE COMPLETELY GONE. YOU WILL FEEL CALMER AND MORE RELAXED.

YOU WILL ALSO FIND THAT IT'S VERY HELPFUL FOR YOU TO START BUILDING A NEW HABIT. THIS TIME, A GOOD HABIT. KEEP A GLASS OF WATER OR GUM, ETC., ALWAYS HANDY, ALWAYS AROUND YOU AS OFTEN AS YOU CAN AND WHENEVER AND WHEREVER YOU CAN, SO THAT YOU CAN LEISURELY SIP ON THAT COOL, REFRESHING WATER, INSTEAD OF REACHING FOR A CIGARETTE LIKE YOU DID IN THE PAST.

YOU ARE NOW GOING TO REACH FOR A GLASS OF WATER OR GUM, ETC. SO ALWAYS KEEP A GLASS OF WATER HANDY OR GUM OR MINTS, ETC. ANYTIME YOU SEE OR HEAR WATER YOU FEEL CALM AND RELAXED.

REACHING FOR A GLASS OF WATER OR GUM, MINTS, OR WHATEVER YOU WISH TO SUBSTITUTE, INSTEAD OF REACHING FOR A CIGARETTE. YOU WILL FIND THAT IT WILL BE VERY EASY FOR YOU TO BE A NON-SMOKER BECAUSE NOW YOU HAVE REPLACED YOUR BAD OLD HABIT WITH A GOOD, NEW HABIT.

THIS IS A GOOD HABIT AND MAKES YOU FEEL IN CONTROL. ANYTIME YOU SEE OR HEAR WATER YOU FEEL CALM AND RELAXED. THIS IS A GOOD HABIT AND MAKES YOU FEEL IN CONTROL. DRINKING WATER OFF AND ON DURING THE DAY OR CHEWING GUM OR A MINT IS A GOOD HABIT AND MAKES YOU FEEL IN CONTROL.

ANYTIME YOU SEE OR HEAR WATER YOU FEEL CALM AND RELAXED. *(repeat)*

ANYTIME YOU ARE AROUND OTHER PEOPLE THAT ARE SMOKING, YOU REALIZE HOW FOOLISH THEY ARE. WHEN YOU SEE OTHER PEOPLE SMOKE IT MAKES YOU ALL THE MORE DETERMINED NOT TO SMOKE. IT ACTUALLY MAKES YOU MORE DETERMINED THAT YOU WANT NOTHING TO DO WITH IT. YOU DO NOT WANT TO SMOKE. ANYTIME THAT YOU SEE SOMEONE ELSE SMOKING IT MAKES YOUR DESIRE TO BE A NON-SMOKER ALL THE STRONGER.

YOU WILL NOT GAIN WEIGHT. YOU WILL ENJOY FOOD MORE BECAUSE YOUR TASTE BUDS WILL BE ABLE TO PICK UP TASTES AND FLAVORS THAT YOU HAVEN'T HAD FOR A LONG TIME. YOU WILL ACTUALLY ENJOY THE TASTE OF FOOD MORE, BUT YOU WILL NOT EAT MORE. YOU WILL ONLY EAT WHEN YOU ARE HUNGRY, AND YOU WILL STOP WHEN YOU ARE SATISFIED, AND NO LONGER FEEL HUNGRY. YOU DO NOT GAIN WEIGHT. YOUR THYROID AND METABOLISM REMAIN THE SAME SO THAT YOU DO NOT GAIN WEIGHT. YOUR METABOLISM STAYS THE SAME, SO YOU DO NOT GAIN WEIGHT. YOUR THYROID AND METABOLISM REMAIN THE SAME SO YOU WILL NOT GAIN WEIGHT AS A NON-SMOKER.

IT MAKES YOU FEEL GOOD TO GET THE COMPLIMENTS AND PATS ON THE BACK AND THE APPROVAL OF YOUR FAMILY AND FRIENDS AND CO-WORKERS BY BEING A NON-SMOKER.

PEOPLE ARE GIVING YOU A LOT OF CREDIT FOR HAVING ACCOMPLISHED THIS. THEY LOOK UP TO YOU,

THOSE THAT ARE STILL SMOKING LOOK UP TO YOU BECAUSE YOU HAVE BEEN ABLE TO STOP. YOU FEEL GOOD ABOUT YOURSELF, AND YOUR FAMILY AND FRIENDS FEEL GOOD ABOUT YOU. THEY'RE PROUD OF YOU, AND YOU DESERVE TO FEEL PROUD OF YOURSELF. YOU NOW BELONG TO THE GROUP THAT IS THE MAJORITY.

WHEN YOU WERE A CHILD IT WAS THE COOL THING TO BE A SMOKER, BUT NOW BECAUSE OF THE HEALTH FACTOR THAT HAS BEEN DISCOVERED, IT'S NOT THE COOL THING TO BE A SMOKER. PEOPLE TEND TO STAND BACK AND SHY AWAY FROM PEOPLE WHO ARE SMOKING. THEY FIND IT UNPLEASANT.

A SMOKER HAS A SMOKE SMELL CLINGING TO THEM. THEIR HOME SMELLS LIKE IT. THEY'RE CLOTHES SMELL OF SMOKE. FOR THOSE WHO ARE NON-SMOKERS, THEY ARE VERY AWARE OF THIS. SO YOU FEEL GOOD ABOUT YOURSELF. YOU DESERVE TO.

NOW AS I COUNT FROM ONE TO FIVE, YOU COME UP MORE AND MORE TO ALERTNESS, FEELING WIDER AND WIDERAWAKE. FEELING MORE REFRESHED, AS THOUGH YOU'VE HAD A NICE, LONG, REFRESHING NAP. ONE . . . COMING UP MORE AND MORE . . . TWO . . . FEELING MORE REFRESHED . . . THREE, FEELING WIDER-AWAKE. FOUR. MORE ALERT AND FIVE. COMPLETELY AWAKE, ALERT, REFRESHED AND OPEN YOUR EYES IN YOUR OWN TIME.

Giving suggestions to stop smoking or anything else is only about 15% effective. Even if it worked it will not usually be permanent, at least not without replacing it with food and becoming overweight.

The only way to get permanent results is to do Regression Therapy to resolve and eliminate what has caused the problem.

POST-HYPNOTIC SUGGESTION FOR STOP SMOKING OR WEIGHT LOSS

Before you count the Stop Smoking subject out of hypnosis give the following Post Hypnotic Suggestion: (it can be adjusted for weight patients also.)

"NOW WE ARE IN PERFECT CONTACT WITH YOUR SUBCONSCIOUS MIND AND WITH YOU FINDING MY VOICE INCREASINGLY COMFORTING, HELPFUL, AND RELAXING. YOU ARE NOW GOING TO ENCODE THE FOLLOWING POSTHYPNOTIC SUGGESTION INTO YOUR SUBCONSCIOUS MIND FOR YOUR SELECTIVE USE WHENEVER YOU DESIRE IT. YOU WILL, FROM THIS MOMENT FORWARD, BE ABLE TO INVOKE THE UNLIMITED POWER OF YOUR SUBCONSCIOUS MIND ANYTIME AND ANYPLACE YOU WANT. SHOULD YOU HAVE THE IDEA YOU WANT TO, *(mention whatever the habit is)*

ALL YOU WILL HAVE TO DO FROM THIS MOMENT FORWARD TO SIGNAL YOUR SUBCONSCIOUS MIND INTO ACTION IS TO TAKE THREE LONG DEEP BREATHS OF CLEAN FRESH AIR, AND YOU WILL FEEL THIS FAR MORE SATISFYING THAN IF YOU HAD JUST HAD SMOKED A CIGARETTE.
(for weight suggest licking their lips three times).

YOU WILL FIND WITH MORE AND MORE CERTAINTY THAT THIS SIMPLE ACTION OF TAKING THREE DEEP BREATHS OF CLEAN FRESH AIR, THAT WHENEVER THE THOUGHT, DESIRE, OR CONTROL YOU WISH TO EVOKE WILL COME SURGING UP FROM THE UNLIMITED STOREHOUSES OF YOUR SUBCONSCIOUS MIND.

YOU FIND THAT YOU WILL BE ABLE TO RELIEVE ANY DISCOMFORT, TENSION, OR UNDESIRABLE URGES. YOU WILL, WITH DAILY INCREASING SUCCESS, BE ABLE TO TAP INTO THE UNLIMITED RESOURCES OF YOUR MEMORIES, TALENTS, AND ABILITIES, WHICH GOD HAS GIVEN YOU TO USE.

NOW, TAKE A NICE LONG DEEP BREATH, AND FEEL THE FRESH, CLEAN, COOL AIR AND HOW IT GOES DEEPLY INTO YOUR LUNGS. GOOD, NOW TAKE ANOTHER GOOD LONG DEEP BREATH. BREATHE IN THE COOL, REFRESHING, CLEAN AIR. EXCELLENT. NOW TAKE ONE MORE GOOD LONG DEEP BREATH AND NOTICE NOW HOW GOOD IT FEELS TO BREATH COOL REFRESHING AIR! NOTICE HOW THE SIGNAL IS BEING PROGRAMMED INTO ALL LEVELS OF YOUR MIND. FEEL THE MESSAGE BEING ACCEPTED AND STRENGTHENED FOR YOUR USE WHENEVER YOU WANT IT. CLEAN REFRESHING AIR IS THE ONLY THING YOU FIND YOU WISH TO BREATHE INTO YOUR LUNGS.
(For weight substitute the suggestion of licking their lips in place of taking breaths of air).

NOW, PLEASE REPEAT OUT LOUD WHAT WILL YOU BE DOING FROM NOW ON TO BE ABLE TO TAP INTO THE UNLIMITED RESOURCES OF YOUR POWERFUL SUBCONSCIOUS MIND TO BE ABLE TO ELIMINATE ANY DESIRE FOR YOUR PAST HABIT." *(Pause)* . . . "VERY GOOD!"

(Have them repeat this two more times. The more often you do this the stronger the suggestion becomes.)

YOU WILL ALSO FIND THAT ANY TIME YOU SEE OR HEAR WATER IN ANY SHAPE OR FORM THAT IT WILL GIVE YOU A VERY SOOTHING, PEACEFUL, RELAXED FEELING. **(Repeat this to client two more times.)**

Giving suggestions to stop smoking or anything else is only about 15% effective. Even if it worked it will not usually be permanent, at least not without replacing it with food and becoming overweight.

The only way to get permanent results is to do Regression Therapy to resolve and eliminate what has caused the problem.

Make a re-enforcement CD for your client to listen to every day between sessions. This will keep re-enforcing the suggestions and will get much better results.

If you wish to purchase CDs for Smoking, Weight Loss, Confidence, to resolve Depression with the Depression Therapy, or a Regression Therapy (which can be used to eliminate the feelings and emotions that cause any problem, that Dr. Gisellla Zukausky made you can order them by e-mail gzukausky@gmail.com or phone (260)484-6727 or write.

Midwest Training Institute of Hypnosis
1504 Kenwood Ave.
Fort Wayne, IN 46805

INCORRECT EATING HABITS LIST

I make a copy of this next page for my weight clients and go over it with them. I instruct them to read the underlined areas before each meal for the next 30 days, till they have changed the bad habits.

I give them a hypnotic re-enforcement tape or CD to listen to each day for the first two weeks. Thereafter I have them listen to it three times a week.

You can make a tape for your client by making it from the SLIM AND TRIM script. Don't be afraid to change or alter the script if you like.

I tell them to not bring junk food or the foods that they crave into the house. They can still eat those foods if they feel they want to when they are away from home, but not to have it around to tempt them at home.

Sometimes they say that someone in the household insists on having junk food around in spite of the fact they have asked them not to. I then tell them to let the other person know that they have got to keep it out of your sight or you will throw it away. That may seem harsh but it is inconsiderate of someone else to be so selfish and make it hard for him or her to avoid junk food. Sometimes others they live with will sabotage their efforts to become slender and more attractive.

I make a small list for them to carry with them of what I have underlined on the next page. I ask them to read it before every meal and then to lay it next to their plate to remind them to change these bad habits.

BAD EATING HABITS YOU CAN CHANGE TO SPEED WEIGHT LOSE

by Dr. Gisella Zukausky, C.Ht.,Ct.H.A.

You can very easily change the bad habits that are also responsible for being overweight. It is best to take a **natural multi vitamin and mineral** each day to make sure you are getting everything you need each day. Otherwise your subconscious keeps sending messages to eat since it is not satisfied. Don't get this anywhere except at a health food store or your chiropractor.

Stop weighing yourself. It is definitely counter productive. Your clothes will tell you your progress. You must start behaving as a normal weight person. They do not weight themselves. They have no reason to.

Be sure to **eat something for breakfast**. If you don't your metabolism slows down and hoards the calories of the food you eat the rest of the day. Also when you finally do eat you will wolf your food.

When you feel hungry don't put off eating for the save reason. If you know for example that you will feel hungry mid morning or mid after noon before you can have a meal then plan ahead for it. Bring sensible snacks from home that you would enjoy eating. Fruit, raw vegetables, protein snack bars, or nuts are good. Protein snack bars and nuts give energy.

Drink a glass of WATER without ice before you start eating. Studies show that you will eat 60%, and will eat slower. When you eat too fast you will be more apt to eat more than you feel comfortable with.

Start with a cup of brothy soup or a cup of salad with low cal dressing. This will also help fill your stomach and cause you to eat much less.
It is best to drink Hot drinks with your meals. Studies show ice drinks coagulates the fats in your food and keeps them longer in your intestines which makes your body absorb them more. Hot drinks with meals are best. You can drink with ice in them and time you are not eating. This will get you faster results.

Before you order or put food on your plate **MAKE A FIST**. This is about the size of your stomach. To satisfy your hunger this is all the food you need. If you still feel somewhat hungry after you eat this amount you can always place a **LITTLE BIT** more on your plate. For the time being always make a fist so you know what you need to put on your plate. Over the years you have gotten in the habit of over loading your plate. In time when it becomes automatic for you to put less on your plate you will not need to keep making a fist to remind yourself. That way you don't need to clean your plate like when you where a child.

Since you are now an adult and don't need to please your parents by eating all the food on your plate make the following rule to yourself. **"I WILL ALWAYS LEAVE SOME FOOD ON MY PLATE SINCE I NO LONGER AM A CHILD."** Then be sure you do. This is to reprogram your mind not to clean your plate.

MOST IMPORTANT STEP IS: To also help you slow down eating so you will not over eat do the following. **Cut your food or take half the size bites** you used to. Chew these smaller bites as long as you would have the larger bites**. After each bite is finished take a sip of your drink**. Hot drinks would be best and give you the quickest results. Keep repeating the steps in this paragraph till you are done eating. After 30 days when you have automatically slowed down your eating you don't have to take a drink after each bite.

When you realize you are feeling satisfied and are done eating but there is still food on your plate do the following: If there is quite a bit of food left **ask for a doggy bag** to be brought with your food. Put your leftovers in it before you are tempted to keep picking at it. This way you can enjoy your food again when you feel hungry latter. If there isn't enough to take home then **destroy your food immediately** by putting too much sugar, salt, or pepper on it so it is ruined. This way you will not be tempted to finish it. Think of each bite as 35 calories.

Carbohydrates are like sugar. I ate foods with carbohydrates **half as often**, such as corn, potatoes, hard beans, and anything with flour in it. If I ever ate bread it was pumpernickel. When I did eat **foods with carbs I ate only half or less** than what I normally did. I ate as much food of other foods as I wanted. That was the only change I made. I was surprised that after 30 days I had lost 10 pounds. I never felt deprived of food. I just ate more of anything else. When eating a sandwich I used only one slice but twice as much filling.

I make copies of this sheet and give each patient one to carry with them to read before eating when they are away from home. It is an outline of the previous page.

Eat something for breakfast.
When you feel hungry, don't put off eating
Eat a sensible snack
Drink one glass of water before eating. No Ice.
MAKE A FIST before putting food on plate.
Start with a cup of bothy soup or salad.
ALWAYS leave some food on plate.
SMALLER BITES and chew longer.
Sip of hot drink after each bite.
Get doggy bag right away. Or destroy food.
Cut back on eating starches.

Eat something for breakfast.
When you feel hungry, don't put off eating
Eat a sensible snack
Drink one glass of water before eating. No Ice.
MAKE A FIST before putting food on plate.
Start with a cup of bothy soup or salad.
ALWAYS leave some food on plate.
SMALLER BITES and chew longer.
Sip of hot drink after each bite.
Get doggy bag right away. Or destroy food.
Cut back on eating starches.

Eat something for breakfast.
When you feel hungry, don't put off eating
Eat a sensible snack
Drink one glass of water before eating. No Ice.
MAKE A FIST before putting food on plate.
Start with a cup of bothy soup or salad.
ALWAYS leave some food on plate.
SMALLER BITES and chew longer.
Sip of hot drink after each bite.
Get doggy bag right away. Or destroy food.
Cut back on eating starches.

Eat something for breakfast.
When you feel hungry, don't put off eating
Eat a sensible snack
Drink one glass of water before eating. No Ice.
MAKE A FIST before putting food on plate.
Start with a cup of bothy soup or salad.
ALWAYS leave some food on plate.
SMALLER BITES and chew longer.
Sip of hot drink after each bite.
Get doggy bag right away. Or destroy food.
Cut back on eating starches.

SLIM AND TRIM SCRIPT

(This can be put on a CD to give to the patient to listen to each day as a re-enforcement.)

NOW THAT YOU ARE IN A SAFE, COMFORTABLE PLACE, I WOULD LIKE YOU TO PICK A SPOT ABOVE EYE LEVEL ON THE CEILING AND JUST CONTINUE TO STARE AT THAT SPOT. YOU WILL NOTICE THAT AS YOU ARE STARING AT THAT SPOT YOUR EYES ARE GETTING HEAVIER AND HEAVIER, MORE AND MORE TIRED. IF AT ANY TIME IT FEELS RIGHT AND COMFORTABLE TO YOU, YOU CAN JUST ALLOW YOUR EYES TO CLOSE AND RELAX. I AM GOING TO COUNT FROM FIVE DOWN TO ONE AND WITH EVERY NUMBER THAT I COUNT YOUR EYES WILL GET MUCH HEAVIER, MUCH DROOPIER, MORE DROWSY. IF YOUR EYES ARE STILL OPEN AT THE COUNT OF ONE, THEN JUST CLOSE THEM AND ALLOW THEM TO RELAX. FIVE . . . YOUR EYES ARE GETTING VERY HEAVY, VERY TIRED. FOUR . . . YOUR EYES ARE GETTING DROOPIER AND DROOPIER. THREE . . . YOUR EYES ARE GETTING VERY HEAVY NOW, VERY DROOPY AND VERY TIRED. TWO . . . VERY HEAVY, VERY TIRED. ONE . . .

NOW JUST ALLOW YOUR EYES TO CLOSE AND RELAX AND SEND ALL OF THAT RELAXATION THROUGH AND AROUND YOUR EYES ALL THE WAY DOWN THROUGH YOUR BODY TO THE VERY TIPS OF YOUR TOES. NOW I'D LIKE YOU TO TAKE A NICE, LONG DEEP BREATH . . . IN THROUGH YOUR NOSE AND EXHALE COMPLETELY THROUGH YOUR MOUTH, JUST GOING DEEPER AND DEEPER RELAXED . . . GOOD. NOW I'D LIKE YOU TO TAKE ANOTHER REAL LONG DEEP BREATH, IN THROUGH YOUR NOSE AND AGAIN EXHALE IT THROUGH YOUR MOUTH. JUST LETTING GO OF ALL STRESS. EXCELLENT. NOW I'D LIKE YOU TO TAKE ANOTHER VERY LONG DEEP BREATH. ALL THE WAY IN THROUGH YOUR NOSE AND HOLD IT FOR THE COUNT OF THREE AND THEN LET IT ALL THE WAY OUT.

YOU CAN FEEL YOURSELF GOING DEEPER AND DEEPER RELAXED, WITH EVERY BREATH THAT YOU EXHALE. ANY SOUND THAT YOU MAY HEAR IN THIS ROOM OR OUT SIDE THIS ROOM, REASSURES YOU THAT EVERYTHING IS NORMAL AND THEREFORE EVERY SOUND WILL FADE INTO THE BACKGROUND. EVERY SOUND WILL GUIDE YOU DEEPER AND DEEPER RELAXED.

FROM NOW ON YOU ARE GOING TO EAT, ACT, AND THINK LIKE A NORMAL WEIGHT PERSON. WHEN YOU ARE HUNGRY YOU EAT. WHEN YOU ARE SATISFIED YOU STOP. THIS MEANS THAT YOU CAN HAVE ANYTHING THAT YOU WANT TO EAT. SINCE YOU ARE EATING LIKE A NORMAL WEIGHT PERSON YOU PREFER FOOD THAT ARE MEANT FOR NORMAL WEIGHT AND GOOD HEALTH.

YOU ARE TUNED INTO WHAT YOUR BODY NEEDS. YOU INSTINCTLY KNOW WHAT YOUR BODY NEEDS. ALL ANIMALS KNOW INSTINCTLY WHAT THEY NEED TO EAT. SOME ARE MEAT EATERS, SOME GRAZE. YOU DON'T HAVE ANY CRAVINGS FOR ANY PARTICULAR FOOD. YOU ONLY DESIRE FOODS YOUR BODY NEEDS.

BY NOW GIVING YOURSELF PERMISSION TO EAT ANYTHING YOU WANT, YOU WILL FIND THAT IN VERY SHORT PERIOD OF TIME YOU ARE GOING TO EAT JUNK FOODS LESS AND LESS. WHEN YOU DO DECIDE TO EAT THEM A LITTLE BIT IS GOING TO SATISFY YOU. SO THE FIRST THING YOU MUST DO IS CHANGE YOUR MENTAL THINKING IN REGARD TO FOOD. YOU MUST START ACTING AND THINKING AS A NORMAL WEIGHT PERSON BY NOT THINKING ABOUT SHOULD AND SHOULD-NOT ANYMORE. YOU ELIMINATE THE WORRY ABOUT FOOD. YOU CAN HAVE ANYTHING YOU WANT JUST LIKE ANY NORMAL WEIGHT PERSON. YOU WILL NOTICE THAT YOU ARE MAKING HEALTHIER CHOICES. SINCE YOU ARE ACTING AND THINKING AS A NORMAL WEIGHT PERSON YOU HAVE NO DESIRE TO HAVE ANY KIND OF JUNK FOOD AT HOME. YOU DESIRE TO HAVE ONLY HEALTHY SNACKS AT HOME. YOU CAN HAVE JUNK FOOD WHEN YOU ARE AWAY FROM HOME BUT YOU WANT ONLY GOOD, HEALTHY FOOD AT HOME. YOU FIND THAT WHEN YOU EAT JUNK FOOD WHEN YOU ARE AWAY FROM HOME YOU ARE SATISFIED WITH ONLY A SMALL AMOUNT.

YOU PROBABLY WILL FIND THAT IF YOU HAVE A PIECE OF PIE FOR EXAMPLE YOU MAY LEAVE OFF THE TOP CRUST AND EAT MOSTLY THE FILLING. YOU REALIZE THAT THIS WILL SAME ABOUT ONE HUMDRED CALORIES. YOU DO THE SAME WHEN YOU DECIDE TO EAT CAKE. YOU LEAVE MOST OF THE FROSTING OFF. YOU NOTICE YOU MAKE THESE HEALTHIER CHOICES NOW. THIS WAY YOU NEVER FEEL DEPRIVED.

YOU FIND THAT YOU DESIRE HEALTHIER FOODS. YOU ARE NOT DIETING. YOU ARE JUST EATING HEALTHIER.

YOU ARE GOING TO TAKE WEIGHT OFF. YOU ARE GOING TO GET DOWN TO YOUR NORMAL SIZE OR WEIGHT. YOU ARE NOW GETTING MORE IN TUNE TO YOUR MECHANISMS OF HUNGER. IF YOU RESPOND TO YOUR NORMAL GOD-GIVEN MECHANISMS IN REGARD TO HUNGER AND THIRST, YOU WILL BECOME NORMAL WEIGHT YOU ARE GETTING MORE AND MORE IN TOUCH AND ARE AWARE OF ALL YOUR BODY'S NATURAL MECHANISMS IN REGARD TO HUNGER AND THIRST, JUST LIKE A NORMAL WEIGHT PERSON. WHEN YOU ARE HUNGRY YOU ASK YOURSELF, "WHAT DO I FEEL LIKE EATING?" YOU WILL AUTOMATICALLY KNOW WHAT THE PROPER FOOD IS THAT YOU FEEL LIKE EATING.

YOUR STOMACH IS THE SIZE OF A FIST, THEREFORE, YOU PUT THIS AMOUNT AND ONLY THIS AMOUNT ON YOUR PLATE TO BEGIN WITH, AND YOU MAKE

IT LAST FOR THE PERIOD OF THE TIME THAT YOU ARE GOING TO BE EATING. IF AFTER THAT TIME YOU STILL FEEL HUNGRY, YOU CAN PUT A FEW MORE SPOONSFUL ON YOUR PLATE. USUALLY THAT WILL BE ENOUGH TO SATISFY YOU. YOU WILL DO THIS UNTIL YOU HAVE RETRAINED YOURSELF TO PUT THE PROPER AMOUNT OF FOOD ON YOUR PLATE.

WHEN YOU FEEL SATISFIED AND NO LONGER HUNGRY, YOU STOP. NO ONE AND NOTHING CAN MAKE YOU EAT ANY MORE. YOU WILL BE JUST LIKE A NORMAL WEIGHT PERSON. YOU CAN EAT AS MUCH AS YOU NEED TO SATISFY YOURSELF BUT TO START OUT YOU PUT THE AMOUNT ON THE PLATE, WHICH IS THE SIZE OF YOUR FIST. SO YOU ALWAYS MAKE A FIST AND THIS WILL REMIND YOU AND HELP YOU TO PUT THE PROPER AMOUNT ON YOUR PLATE. THERE IS NO NEED TO PUT MORE ON YOUR PLATE, BECAUSE YOUR STOMACH WILL FEEL COMFORTABLE WITH THIS AMOUNT.

MORE FOOD WILL MAKE YOU FEEL STUFFED AND UNCOMFORTABLE, BECAUSE IT WILL STRETCH YOUR STOMACH AND THAT WILL MAKE YOU FEEL UNCOMFORTABLE IF YOU EAT ANY MORE AFTER YOU ARE SATISFIED. WHEN YOU SEE SOMEONE ELSE FILL THEIR PLATE AND STUFF FOOD DOWN YOU SEE HOW FOOLISH THEY ARE, THEREFORE YOU ARE ALL THE MORE DETERMINED TO EAT NORMALLY AND COMFORTABLY. IT IS NORMAL TO BE NORMAL WEIGHT. YOU ARE GOING TO DO WHAT IS PERFECTLY NORMAL TO DO. THAT IS WHY IT WILL BE EASY FOR YOU TO EAT IN THIS MANNER. WHEN YOU NO LONGER FEEL HUNGRY AND FEEL SATISFIED, YOU WILL STOP EATING. NO ONE OR NOTHING CAN MAKE YOU EAT ONE BITE MORE. YOU WILL FEEL SATISFIED. YOU HAVE NO DESIRE TO EAT ANY MORE.

YOU WILL NOTICE YOU EAT JUNK FOODS LESS AND LESS OFTEN AND WHEN YOU DO EAT THEM YOU WILL NO LONGER FEEL GUILTY WHEN YOU EAT THEM, LIKE A NORMAL WEIGHT PERSON, AND A LITTLE WILL SATISFY YOU. IT IS NATURAL TO BE NORMAL WEIGHT. THEREFORE IT WILL BE VERY EASY FOR YOU TO BE A NORMAL WEIGHT PERSON. IT IS UNNATURAL FOR YOU TO BE OVERWEIGHT AND TO EAT MORE THAN WHAT YOUR STOMACH FEELS COMFORTABLE WITH.

YOUR METABOLISM WILL FUNCTION MORE EFFICIENTLY SO THAT YOU WILL USE UP CALORIES FASTER, FROM THE FOOD YOU EAT EACH DAY UNTIL YOU REACH YOUR PROPER WEIGHT AND THEN YOU'RE METABOLISM WILL STABILIZE. BY GETTING IN TOUCH WITH YOUR BODY'S MECHANISMS AND ASKING YOURSELF "WHAT DO I FEEL LIKE EATING?" WHEN YOU'RE HUNGRY, YOU WILL BECOME AWARE THAT YOU ENJOY FRUITS AND VEGETABLES MORE THAN YOU EVER HAVE BEFORE. AND THAT YOU WILL BE EATING THEM MORE. FRUITS AND VEGETABLES GIVE YOU MORE ENERGY. FRUIT IS GOD'S DESERT FOR US THAT HE HAS PROVIDED.

THIS IS WHY WE EAT FOOD. IT IS FOR ENERGY. THIS IS WHAT HUMAN BEINGS WERE DESIGNED TO EAT, ESPECIALLY RAW FRUITS AND VEGETABLES. YOU WILL NOTICE THAT WHEN YOU EAT THESE FOODS YOU FEEL BETTER AND HAVE MORE ENERGY. YOU WANT TO EAT THEM MORE. THAT IS BECAUSE

WHEN YOU EAT THESE FOODS YOU FEEL BETTER PHYSICALLY AND EMOTIONALLY. YOU FEEL LIGHTER. FOOD IS CHEMICALS AND WHEN YOU EAT THE FOODS THAT ARE NATURAL FOR YOU AND MAKE US FEEL BETTER EMOTIONALLY AND PHYSICALLY; YOU WANT THEM MORE AND MORE OFTEN.

WHEN YOU FEEL HUNGERY BUT IT ISN'T MEAL TIME YOU DO NOT DEPRIVE YOUR BODY. YOU EAT A LITTLE BIT OF A HEALTHY SNACK, SUCH AS FRUIT OR VEGITABLES, ESPECIALLY WHEN THEY ARE RAW BECAUSE YOU LIKE THE CRUNCH OF THEM. YOU ALSO ALWAYS KEEP NUTS AROUND. NUTS ARE PROTIEN WHICH IS LIKE GAS TO OUR CARS. IT GIVE US THE MOST ENERGY.

YOU WILL YOU BE DRAWN INSTINCTIVELY TO THE FOODS THAT MAKE YOU FEEL BETTER. YOU ALSO WILL BE IN TOUCH WITH YOUR MECHANISM OF THIRST. WHEN YOU FEEL THIRSTY YOUR BODY RECOGNIZES ONLY PLAIN, PURE WATER. ANY TIME YOU FEEL THIRSTY, YOU INSTINCTIVELY AND AUTOMATICALLY GIVE YOUR BODY A DRINK OF WATER FIRST BEFORE ANYTHING ELSE.

YOU THINK, ACT AND DO WHAT A NORMAL WEIGHT PERSON WOULD. YOU ARE THINKING OF YOURSELF AS A NORMAL WEIGHT PERSON NOW. YOU IMAGINE YOURSELF AS A NORMAL WEIGHT PERSON, AND THE WEIGHT THAT YOU WANT TO BE. YOU CLOSE YOUR EYES AND YOU IMAGINE YOURSELF AS BEING THAT WEIGHT ALREADY. YOU WILL DO THIS SEVERAL TIMES A DAY.

I WOULD LIKE NOW TO TALK TO YOUR SUBCONSCIOUS MIND. I WANT TO TALK DIRECTLY TO YOUR SUBCONSCIOUS MIND. THE REASONS THAT YOU HAVE CAUSED THIS EXTRA WEIGHT ARE IN THE PAST. THESE REASONS NO LONGER EXIST IN THE PRESENT. IT WILL NEVER HAPPEN AGAIN. YOU HAVE FOUND BETTER WAYS OF DEALING WITH THESE ISSUES INSTEAD OF EATING EXCESSIVELY. YOU DON'T HAVE TO BE AFRAID ANY MORE OF WHAT IT WAS THAT CAUSED YOU TO BE OVERWEIGHT. YOU ARE GROWN UP AND OLDER NOW. YOU ARE IN CONTROL AND IN CHARGE OF YOUR LIFE NOW. YOU ARE AN ADULT. YOU ARE GROWN UP AND NO ONE CAN TELL YOU TO DO OR SAY ANYTHING THAT YOU DON'T WANT TO. YOU ARE IN CONTROL OF YOUR LIFE. YOU ARE AN ADULT NOW.

THE ONLY TIME THAT YOU ARE NOT IS WHEN YOU GIVE THAT CONTROL TO SOMEONE ELSE. YOU HAVE TO DELIBERATELY GIVE IT TO SOMEONE ELSE IF YOU ARE NOT IN CONTROL. THEREFORE, YOU DON'T HAVE TO BE AFRAID OF WHAT CAUSED YOU TO BE OVERWEIGHT. YOU CAN MAKE GOOD, HONEST,

RATIONAL, SMART DECISIONS FOR YOURSELF. YOU HAVE LEARNED BETTER WAYS OF DEALING WITH THE ISSUES.

IT IS NOW O.K. FOR YOU TO BE NORMAL WEIGHT. IT IS NOW SAFE FOR YOU TO BE NORMAL WEIGHT. HEAR ALL THE DIFFERENT COMMENTS THAT PEOPLE ARE SAYING TO COMPLEMENT YOU AS YOU IMAGINE YOURSELF NORMAL WEIGHT NOW. THE MORE YOU FOCUS ON YOU AS A NORMAL WEIGHT PERSON, THE MORE YOUR SUBCONSCIOUS MAKES IT A REALITY.

YOU WILL BE CALM AND RELAXED BECAUSE YOU WILL BE IN CONTROL OF YOUR EATING. YOU ARE EATING NORMALLY NOW. EATING WHAT YOU FEEL LIKE EATING. YOU ARE EATING NATURALLY LIKE GOD INTENDED. YOU WANT TO EAT ONLY HEALTHY FOOD AND ONLY IN THE COMFORTABLE AMOUNT THAT SATISFIES YOU. YOU ENJOY AND SAVOR YOUR FOOD SO YOU EAT VERY SLOWLY NOW. EATING SLOWLY MAKES YOU APPRECIATE THE GOOD TASTE OF YOUR FOOD MORE. YOU WILL NEVER GAIN YOUR WEIGHT BACK THAT YOU HAVE TAKEN OFF. NOR DO YOU FALL BACK INTO THE OLD THINKING OF AN OVERWEIGHT PERSON. YOU MUST ACT, THINK, AND FEEL ABOUT FOOD AS A NORMAL WEIGHT PERSON. YOU WILL
CONTINUE TO EAT ANYTHING YOU WANT AND ONLY WHEN YOU ARE HUNGRY AND STOP WHEN YOU ARE SATISFIED. YOU CONTINUE TO MAKE A FIST WHEN YOU SIT DOWN TO EAT AND PUT ONLY THAT AMOUNT ON YOUR PLATE.

WHEN YOU ARE HUNGRY BETWEEN MEALS YOU ALWAYS HAVE HEALTHY SNACK AROUND WEATHER IT IS AT HOME OR AT WORK.

YOU NOW KEEP A GLASS OF WATER NEAR YOU, WHENEVER POSSIBLE. THIS IS YOUR NEW HABIT TO REPLACE YOUR HABIT OF EATING IMPROPERLY OR DRINKING UNHEALTHY BEVERAGES LIKE POP. IT IS A GOOD HABIT. IT IS A HEALTHY HABIT. THIS HABIT OF REACHING FOR YOUR WATER AND LEISURELY SIPPING ON THAT REFRESHING DRINK OF WATER, WILL REPLACE YOUR HABIT OF EATING EXCESSIVELY OR DRINKING UNHEALTHY DRINKS.

IT MAKES YOU FEEL BETTER THAN EATING EXCESSIVELY DID, BECAUSE YOU FEEL MORE IN CONTROL. YOU FEEL MORE IN CHARGE OF THINGS AND OF YOURSELF.

IT GIVES YOU A GOOD FEELING. YOU FEEL GOOD ABOUT YOURSELF WHEN YOU REACH FOR THAT WATER INSTEAD OF FOOD. LEISURELY SIPPING ON THAT COOL, REFRESHING WATER INSTEAD.

YOU ALSO WILL WANT TO DRINK A GLASS OF WATER BEFORE YOU START ANY MEAL, PREFERABLY WITHOUT ICE IF POSSIBLE. YOU WILL FIND THAT BY DOING THIS YOU HAVE LESS NEED TO OVER EAT. IT IS SUCH AN EASY WAY TO NOT OVER EAT.

YOU ALSO WHENEVER YOU CAN EAT A SMALL CUP OF SOUP WITH LOTS OF BROTH OR A SMALL CUP OF SALAD. ALSO YOU WILL FIND THAT IF YOU HAVE HOT DRINKS WITH YOUR MEALS IT WILL CAUSE YOU TO ELIMINATE THE FATS IN YOUR FOOD INSTEAD OF BEING OBSORBED INTO YOUR BODY MORE WITH COLD DRINKS. YOU CAN SAVE THE COLD DRINKS WHEN YOU ARE NOT EATING.

WITH EVERY DAY THAT PASSES, YOU ARE EATING MORE NORMALLY AND FEELING BETTER ABOUT YOURSELF. NOW I WOULD LIKE YOU TO THINK OF A TIME IN THE PAST WHEN YOU WERE COMPLETELY IN CONTROL AND IN CHARGE OF A SITUATION. A TIME WHEN YOU KNEW EXACTLY WHAT TO DO AND EXACTLY WHAT TO SAY. YOU KNEW EXACTLY HOW IT WOULD TURN OUT, AND INDEED IT DID. I WOULD LIKE YOU TO THINK OF SUCH A TIME NOW. NOD YOUR HEAD WHEN YOU REMEMBER. NOW I WOULD LIKE YOU TO INTENSIFY THAT TIME AND THAT EXPERIENCE BY REMEMBERING EVERYTHING YOU HEARD, EVERYTHING YOU SAW, EVERYTHING YOU SAID TO YOURSELF OR TO OTHERS AND ESPECIALLY GET IN TOUCH WITH THOSE GOOD STRONG FEELINGS OF BEING IN CHARGE AND IN CONTROL OF THE SITUATION. I WOULD LIKE YOU TO INTENSIFY THAT EXPERIENCE NOW **(PAUSE)** THAT'S RIGHT—VERY GOOD. STAY IN TOUCH WITH THAT GOOD STRONG FEELING OF BEING IN CONTROL AND IN CHARGE. **(PLACE YOUR HAND ON THEIR SHOULDER TO ANCHOR THIS GOOD FEELING, AND THEN REMOVE YOUR HAND.)**

NOW I'D LIKE YOU TO THINK OF A TIME IN THE FUTURE WHEN YOU MIGHT BE THINKING OF EATING SOME FOOD BUT YOU DON'T REALLY WANT TO AND DON'T FEEL LIKE YOU NEED TO. NOD WHEN YOU HAVE SUCH A TIME IN MIND. AS YOU THINK ABOUT THAT FOOD, SAY TO YOURSELF, "NO! I DON'T NEED THAT". **(PLACE YOUR HAND ON THE SAME SPOT AGAIN TO ANCHOR THE GOOD FEELING OF BEING IN CONTROL AGAIN)**

FEEL THOSE GOOD FEELINGS OF BEING IN CHARGE AND IN CONTROL. **(NOW TAKE YOUR HAND OFF)**.

NOW I'D LIKE YOU TO THINK OF ANOTHER TIME IN THE FUTURE THAT YOU MIGHT BE THINKING OF FOOD YOU WANT TO EAT. YOU KNOW YOU AREN'T REALLY HUNGRY AND YOU DON'T REALLY WANT TO EAT. NOD YOUR HEAD WHEN YOU THINK OF SUCH TIME AS YOU THINK ABOUT THE FOOD YOU MIGHT WANT TO EAT, SAY TO YOURSELF **(PLACE HAND ON SHOULDER)**, "NO, I DON'T NEED THAT". AS YOU SAY THOSE WORDS TO YOURSELF, FEEL THE GOOD STRONG FEELINGS OF BEING IN CHARGE AND IN CONTROL AGAIN. NOD YOUR HEAD WHEN YOU FEEL THOSE GOOD FEELINGS. **(NOW REMOVE HAND)**
NOW I'D LIKE YOU TO THINK OF ANOTHER TIME IN THE FUTURE. YOU MIGHT BE THINKING ABOUT FOOD THAT YOU WANT TO EAT, BUT YOU'D REALLY RATHER NOT EAT. NOD YOUR HEAD WHEN YOU HAVE SUCH A TIME. AS YOU THINK ABOUT THAT FOOD, SAY TO YOURSELF CLEARLY **(PLACE HAND ON**

SHOULDER), "NO I DON'T NEED THAT". FEEL THOSE GOOD STRONG FEELINGS OF BEING IN CHARGE AND IN CONTROL TAKE OVER.

ANYTIME IN THE FUTURE THAT YOU WANT TO FEEL THAT CONTROL, ALL YOU NEED TO DO IS SAY TO YOURSELF CLEARLY, "NO I DON'T NEED THAT", AND THOSE GOOD FEELINGS OF BEING IN CHARGE AND IN CONTROL WILL TAKE OVER. **(REMOVE HAND)**

NOW YOU CAN GIVE YOURSELF PERMISSION FOR YOU TO BE NORMAL WEIGHT AGAIN. I WANT YOU TO THINK THIS TO YOURSELF VERY CLEARLY AND REPEAT IT TO YOURSELF THREE TIMES THAT IT IS O.K. AND ALL RIGHT FOR YOU TO BE NORMAL WEIGHT AGAIN. YOUR METABOLISM WILL ADJUST TO CONSUME YOUR CALORIE INTAKE EACH DAY MORE RAPIDLY. IT WILL ADJUST TO A LEVEL THAT WILL STILL BE HEALTHY FOR YOU. AS YOUR WEIGHT COMES OFF MORE AND MORE EACH DAY YOU FIND YOU WILL HAVE MORE ENERGY AND BECOME MORE ACTIVE PHYSICALLY.

AS YOU GET SLIMMER AND TRIMMER YOU FEEL SO MUCH MORE ENERGY THAT YOU DESIDER TO BE MORE PHYSICAL THEN YOU HAVE EVER BEEN. YOU START NOW BY TAKING A BRISK WALK EVERY DAY FOR FIVE OR TEN MINUTES FOR THE FIRST TWO WEEKS. YOU ADD FIVE MINUTES PER DAY EVERY WEEK THERAFTER. YOU SET A TIME EACH DAY THAT YOU WILL DO THIS. IF YOU EVER CHOOSE TO DO A DIFFERENT EXCERSIZE YOU CAN.

NORMALLY SKIN DOES NOT SHRINK AS MUCH AS THE BODY. HOWEVER, YOU WILL BE AMAZED THAT YOUR SKIN DOES SHRINK AS MUCH AS YOU'RE BODY. IN FACT IT WILL BE MORE FIRM AND YOUTHFUL LOOKING, BUT AT A COMFORTABLE LEVEL. YOUR FACE WILL ESPECIALLY HAVE THE SKIN SHRINK TO BE FIRM AND YOUTHFUL. **(Repeat from beginning of this paragraph.)**

NOW AS I COUNT FROM ONE TO FIVE, YOU WILL BE ALERT AND AWAKE. YOU WILL OPEN YOUR EYES COMPLETELY REFRESHED AND ALERT ON THE COUNT OF FIVE, AS THOUGH YOU HAVE HAD A NICE NAP. (Be sure to count very, very, slowly, so they will have plenty of time to fully come out of hypnosis.) ONE . . . . TWO . . . . THREE . . . . FOUR . . FIVE.

Feel free to make changes to suit the needs of your client. As you get more experienced you will feel more confident to write your own scripts. Always be sure to use only positive words and suggestions. ***Do not say what you don't want them to do, only what you want them to do.***

Remember that without getting to the cause of this problem it will only be about 15% successful and then probably not permanent.

TEACH IMAGERY AND AUTOSUGGESTIONS

TO WEIGHT CLIENT

I tell them the following:

"I'D LIKE YOU TO IMAGINE THAT YOU ARE WALKING ALONG YOUR OWN PRIVATE BEAUTIFUL BEACH. YOU CAN BE ALONE OR WITH SOMEONE. NO ONE CAN SEE YOU. AS YOU WALK ALONG THIS BEAUTIFUL BEACH YOU NOTICE THAT AGAINST THE BEAUTIFUL BLUE SKY THE FLUFFY WHITE CLOUDS ARE LAZILY DRIFTING ALONG.

THE PLESANT WARM SUN IS SHINING. YOU SEE THE WHITE CAPS ROLLING IN TO THE SHORE WASHING OVER YOUR BARE FEET, AND IT FEELS SO GOOD. YOU HEAR AND SEE THE SEA GULLS FLYING OFF OVER THE WATER.

THERE IS A COOL BREEZE BLOWING OFF THE WATER, BRUSHING YOUR CHEEKS AND BLOWING THROUGH YOUR HAIR. YOU HEAR THE WIND RUSTLING THE LEAVES IN THE TREES ALONG THE SHORE.

AS YOU WALK ALONG YOU NOTICE THE PLEASANT WARM SUN AS IT IS SHINING ON YOU. WITH EVERY STEP YOUR EXCESS BODY FAT IS MELTING AWAY IN ALL THE RIGHT PLACES, TILL YOU ARE THE SHAPE AND SIZE YOU WANT TO BE. WHEN YOU ARE THE SHAPE AND SIZE YOU WANT TO BE NOD YOUR HEAD.

(When they nod say,) NOW REPEAT AFTER ME: I AM SLENDER, I AM TRIM. I'M LIGHT ON MY FEET AND I FEEL SO GOOD ABOUT MYSELF. **(Have them repeat after you 2 more times. Now say,)** THE MORE TIMES YOU DO THIS MENTAL IMAGERY AND SUGGESTIONS THE SOONER YOUR SUBCONSCIOUS MIND WILL HELP YOU REACH YOUR GOAL. EVERY TIME YOU HAVE A BREAK FOR ONE MINUTE DURING THE DAY DO THIS QUICK MENTAL EXERCISE."

I encourage my patients to do this at least once a day or better yet morning and evening at bed time. Patients that do this reach their normal weight much faster than those who do not.

The subconscious mind does not think so it accepts this as a fact and will react to it making it happen much more quickly.

This is the "Power of Positive Thinking" applied for Weight Loss.

The parts of this book on working with Dental patients and Pregnant women have been taken from parts of the book VISUALIZATION AND GUIDED IMAGERY FOR PAIN MANAGEMENT written by R.D. Longacre, PH.D., F.B.H.A. Who is no longer with us. I have made changes and additions to it.

HOW DOES HYPNOSIS HELP IN DENTAL WORK?

It reduces salivation, and the possibility of shock.

Hypnosis can control bleeding.

It can also help dental patients with broxism and unconscious grinding their teeth.

Helping patient get used to braces or false teeth and feel more comfortable after the patient has agreed to accept them.

Helping patient to be comfortable during long and arduous periods of dental work.

Help eliminate gagging and nausea.

If anesthesia is needed the use of it is reduced when hypnosis is used.

Hypnotic Anesthesia can be substituted for, or in combination with, pre-medication for general anesthesia.

Use a longer induction and taking them to their safe comfortable place and mentioning some of the things they may be doing there while the work is being done.

Postoperative analgesia

Precautions: The major precaution for the use of hypnosis in dentistry is symptomatic pain removal. Professional hypnotherapists should not attempt to deal with symptomatic pain due to oral dysfunction of disease without consulting with a dental physician.

It is best to meet with the dental patient two or three days before their dental appointment. You can make a CD also of the following script of being more and more relaxed and confident when going to the dentist. It would reenforce your suggestions that you made in the office if they listen to it every day including the day of the appointment.

SUGGESTIONS THAT CAN BE GIVEN TO A FRIGHTENED OR FUSSY DENTAL PATIENT

1. After they are hypnotized tell them the following statements: that with every block that they get closer to dentists office they get calmer and more relaxed. They will have confidence in a quick and efficient dental procedure. As they enter the dentist office they become even more comfortable and relaxed.
   As they sit down in the dentist's chair they continue to be calmer and more relaxed.

2. Create amnesia by saying that when the dental work is completed and they are brought out of hypnosis they will feel like they had been hypnotized only 3 minutes and they will feel wonderful throughout their entire body. If dental surgery has been done tell them they bleed only slightly and will heal very quickly.

3. Do the following script and give same suggestions as for Hypno-Anesthesia.

SCRIPT TO HELP DENTAL PATIENT

Hypnosis can readily ameliorate (eliminate) the tension, nervousness and unreasonable fear of pain often exhibited by fussy patients. The hypnotherapist should meet preferably three times just before seeing the dentist. Post hypnotic suggestions are given at this time by doing an induction and saying the following script.

YOU ARE CONFIDENT WHEN YOU GO TO THE DENTIST BECAUSE ON THE DAY OF YOUR APPOINTMENT YOU ARE CALM AND RELAXED. YOU ARE LOOKING FORWARD TO THE DENTIST APPOINTMENT. YOU HAVE TAKEN EXCELLENT CARE OF YOUR TEETH AND GUMS. (say this only if they have taken care of their teeth.)

YOU WILL BE AMAZED HOW MUCH RELAXATION AND WELL BEING YOU FEEL AS YOU DRIVE TO THE DENTIST. WITH EVERY BLOCK YOU GET CLOSER AND CLOSER TO THE DENTISTS OFFICE YOU WILL BE MORE AND MORE RELAXED AND CONFIDENT IN A COMFORTABLE AND RELAXED AND CALM TIME. WHEN YOU ENTER THE DENTISTS OFFICE YOU WILL HAVE A FEELING OF WELL BEING AND CALMNESS COME OVER YOU EVEN MORE THAN BEFORE. YOU WILL BLEED ONLY A SLIGHTLY AND WILL BE AMAZED HOW RAPIDLY YOU HEAL. YOU WILL FEEL GOOD, YOU WILL FEEL GREAT, AND YOU WILL FEEL COMFORTABLE WHEN THE APPOINTMENT IS DONE.

YOU ARE CONFIDENT AND VERY COMFORTABLE WHILE YOU ARE IN THE DENTIST OFFICE. THAT IS YOUR SIGNAL TO BE VERY CALM AND RELAXED. IN FACT THE NIGHT BEFORE YOUR APPOINTMENT YOU ARE LOOKING FORWARD TO THE EXPERIENCE BECAUSE YOU KNOW YOU WILL BE IN GOOD HAND AND VERY WELL TAKEN CARE OF.

WHEN YOU SIT IN THE DENTISTS CHAIR YOU WILL FEEL EVEN MORE RELAXED BECAUSE YOU KNOW YOUR DENTIST IS VERY QUAILIFIED. LET YOURSELF GO TO A COMFORTABLE SAFE PLACE WHEN YOU ARE SITTING IN THE DENTISTS CHAIR. NOD YOUR HEAD WHEN YOU HAVE DECIDED WHERE THAT WILL BE AND WHAT YOU WILL BE DOING AT YOUR SAFE COMFORTABLE PLACE.

CONTINUE TO FEEL CALM KNOWING THAT YOU WILL HAVE A GREAT OUTCOME AND HAVE YOUR TEETH LOOKING GREAT.

(If getting braces or false teeth say:)

THIS NEW APPARATUS IS A GOOD THING FOR YOUR HEALTH. IT FEELS SO NATURAL FOR YOU AS THOUGH YOU'VE WORE THEM FOR YEARS. HAVING THEM IS A STATUS SYMBAL. NOT EVERYONE CAN AFFORD THIS.

HAVE A CONVERSATION NOW WITH YOUR TEETH THAT THIS WILL BE AN EASY AND BRIEF EXPERIENCE FOR YOU. WHEN YOU HAVE TALKED TO YOUR TEETH THAT IT WILL BE AN EASY AND BRIEF EXPERIENCE FOR YOU NOD YOUR HEAD. (When they nod continue.)

WHEN THE DENTAL WORK IS COMPLETED AND YOU ARE BROUGHT OUT OF THIS STATE YOU WILL FEEL LIKE YOU HAD BEEN SITTING HERE FOR ONLY 3 MINUTES AND YOU WILL FEEL WONDERFUL THROUGHOUT YOUR ENTIRE BODY.

(Give same well being suggestions as for Hypno-Anesthesia.)

(Say the following for braces:)

BRACES YOU KNOW ARE ONLY TEMPORARY. IT IS EASY FOR YOU TO WARE YOUR BRACES AND THE TIME TO WEAR THEM WILL PASS QUICKLY AND LEAVE YOU WITH A BEAUTIFUL SMILE.
(now emerge them.)

PROMOTING YOURSELF WITH DENTISTS

It is easier to interest dentists in what we can do to help their patients than it is a doctor. They are more open to hypnosis.

Go to the dentists office and leave reading material and a short cassette tape for them to listen to or a video of dental work being done with hypnosis. Leave it with the person in charge of the office to give to the doctor. Tell them you will be by in one week to pick it up and you would like to briefly talk to the doctor.

In one week call first to see if the doctor has a few minutes to talk to you.

Tell the doctor you will see as many of his fussy or patients that have difficulty as he wants to send to you for $100 (or whatever amount you choose) a month retainer. A dentist usually doesn't have more than 2 or 3 a month. You then charge the patient $25 co-payment when they come to you. Each session shouldn't take more than 30 minutes for the fussy patient. Patients with gag reflex problems etc. about an hour.

Explain to the doctor the procedure is not invasive and reduces the patients tension, fear and anxiety, and this will make his work easier, and will save him time.

INDICATION FOR HYPNOTIC CHILDBIRTH

1. Eliminating fear, tension, and pain before, during and after labor and delivery with a higher pain threshold.
2. Less pain medication will be necessary or even eliminated.
3. Painful uterine contraction that could be experienced during normal labor and delivery can be lessened or eliminated.
4. Decreases shock and recovery is faster.
5. Eliminates or lessens post operative effects
6. Lessens and shortens the first stage of labor as much as three to four hours for first time mothers in their labor and delivery.
7. Hypnosis reduces the fatigue caused by prolonged or difficult labor, allowing the mother to be more alert and aware when their baby is born.
8. Hypnotic rapport can be transferred during the training sessions by telling the patient that any individual participating in the birthing process can help the patient and do not need special training.

Contraindications

Drugs given to the mother during child to the mother to relieve pain can decrease the oxygen supply to the fetus. There is no harm that can come to the baby or mother using hypnosis to lower or eliminate the pain.

Hypnotic Childbirth Instruction

For best results the six sessions should start about the third or fourth month of pregnancy. The number of sessions needed to teach the patient self-hypnosis techniques could vary from one to twenty. Six training sessions before the birth is usually sufficient to have a rewarding birthing experience.

The Hypnotherapist should assess the patient's ability to get at least a medium stage of hypnosis quickly and easily and be able to perform glove anaesthesia at least while in the state of hypnosis.

6 SESSION PROTOCOL FOR TEACHING EXPECTANT MOTHERS PAINLESS CHILDBIRTH

(Some of this was taken from Dr. R.D. Longacre's book, VISUALIZATION AND GUIDED IMAGERY FOR PAIN MANAGEMENT. His book is no longer published because of his passing. I changed much of it that I found more effective.)

1. Session number one

a.) Give them the information flier.

b.) Have them fill out the intake form.

c.) OB/GYN should be advised about his/her patient's desire for hypnotherapy for painless childbirth.

d.) They should listen to a patient education cassette on hypnotic natural childbirth.

e.) Hypnotic childbirth therapist should review the intake form, conduct a clinical interview, perform suggestibility tests and place the patient in a state of hypnosis using the Somnambulisum and Esdaile Scripts.

f.) Therapeutic suggestions given during the first session should be formulated to instill confidence that childbirth will be a normal and natural body process and a joyful experience for the mother-to-be. Suggestions should also be given demonstrate glove anesthesia to the patient and to demonstrate the depth of hypnosis achieved during the 1st visit. (by doing the pinch test as in Somnabulisum Script.

g.) Give Post hypnotic suggestions for self hypnosis as in Somnabulisum Script.

h.) Give Post hypnotic suggestions for rapid induction by you in the future as in the Somnambulism Script.

i.) Tell them that when they do self hypnosis they can test to see if they are deep enough by trying to open their eyes. (WHEN YOU TAKE THREE DEEP BREATHS AND THINK THE WORD RELAX YOU WILL GO INTO THE DEEPEST RELAXED STATE YOU HAVE BEEN IN.)
If they still can not go deep enough to allow more time till they are unable to not able to open their eyes.

j.) Also program them with raising the index finger slowly and saying that will be a yes signal from now on. Do the same with the little finger and say that will be a no signal from now on. Most patients will respond to these signals automatically when they are deep enough that they will feel no pain. Give them the suggestion that from now on that can tell tell themselves just like using their own computer to tell themselves that their yes finger will automatically signal by going up till they feel it when they are at a level of anesthesia in their body. This way they have two ways of knowing when they have achieved that level. If the finger signals are not strong enough they can tell with the eye test. When they know are anesthetized they are told to say yes or OK so others will know they have achieved that level.

k.) Give the suggestion that if they feel they need to deepen their hypnosis that they should say the word <u>Relax</u> three times.

l.) Give the suggestions for Glove Anesthesia. Tell them they can think their hand numb any time even without hypnosis and then be able to transfer the numbness to any part of their body. Use the Glove Anesthesia Script.

m.) Instruct the patient to practice Self Hypnosis and Glove Anesthesia every day at least once.

n.) Tell them that they can emerge themselves from hypnosis by counting from one to five and slowly opening their eyes.

o.) Let them know that if they ever feel groggy or have a dull headache from opening their eyes too quickly they should close their eyes and wait ten to twenty seconds before opening their eyes again.

2. Session number two

a.) Do Rapid Induction. If they do more than just twitch when you ask them to try to lift their arms, legs, and open their eyes, they are not deep enough. Then do the Somnamfulisum Script and the Esdaile script, till they can only twitch and are unable to open their eyes. Again give them Post hypnotic Suggestions for rapid induction from now on.

b.) Have them test their eyes or tell their yes finger to signal when they have reached the level of anesthesia. When they have they are told to say yes or OK so others will know they have achieved that level.

c.) Now natural childbirth suggestions are given.

d.) Lead them to imagine the Hypnotic Childbirth Imagery for comfortable and the joyful experience of them giving birth.

e.) Again give the suggestions for Glove Anesthesia. Tell them they can think their hand numb any time even without hypnosis and then be able to transfer the numbness to any part of their body.

f.) Give Post Hypnotic suggestions for self hypnosis again. (WHEN YOU TAKE THREE DEEP BREATHS AND THINK THE WORD RELAX YOU WILL GO INTO THE DEEPEST RELAXED STATE YOU HAVE BEEN IN.)

g.) Emerge the patient and then ask them to do self hypnosis again and to let you know when they have check their eyes or when they have their finger go up so they will know they are in anesthesia, by saying yes. Do the pinch test to prove to them they are in a state of anesthesia.

h.) Have them do the Glove Anesthesia and then transfer it again.

i.) Give them the Post Hypnotic Suggestion that when their husband or anyone at the time of giving birth can give a gentle squeeze on their wrist with his thumb and index finger she will go into a deeper state of Anesthesia each time.

j.) Give them the Post Hypnotic Suggestion that their husband or anyone at the time of giving birth will put them into a state of hypnosis if need be.

k.) Have them Emerge and then have them re-hypnotize themselves. Also have them deepen the hypnotic state by doing it several times after hypnotizing them.

l.) Give Post Hypnotic Suggestions that reinforces their ability to achieve a deep state of relaxation every time they want to.

m.) Give the suggestion again that if they feel they need to deepen their hypnosis that they should say the word Relax three times.

n.) Tell them to have their husband or couch come the next time.

o.) Build their excitement and enthusiasm for that time and how well they are doing. Reassure them that the results will be really successful and how well they are doing with learning how to do all this.

3. Session number three

a.) The husband or coach are to participate this time.

b.) Ask them to put themselves into the hypnotic state and to say yes when they are there. Tell them again that when their husband or coach gently squeezes their wrist they will be able to go into this state of hypnosis or if they already are hypnotized they will go deeper relaxed.

c.) Give other appropriate Post Hypnotic Suggestions at this time.

d.) Have the patient emerge themselves by counting from one to five, and then to practice their partner hypnotizing them several more times.

4. Session number four

a.) At the end of this session give them a letter for their OB/GYN letting him/her know what you are doing, and that if they have any questions to feel free to call you.

b.) A childbirth reinforcement CD is also given to the patient for home use. This should have a progressive relaxation induction and suggestions that enhance the outcome of individual therapy sessions for success. It should also have suggestions for comfortable, and joyful, easy labor and delivery. Build their excitement and enthusiasm for that time and how well they are doing. Reassure them that the results will be really successful and how well they are doing.

5. Session number five

a.) Instruct the patient for the appropriate time when to use their hypnosis. By doing this it will prevent the possibility of the patient using the self hypnosis too soon that will have them ignore the labor pains when they begin and then having to rush to the hospital.

b.) The best time to start them is after they have arrived at the hospital.

6. Session number six

a.) The sixth session I have the husband again come with the patient and they practice all the skills of self-hypnosis, glove anesthesia and wrist squeezing they have been taught.

Hypnosis can help to keep from having the baby prematurely. Suggestions can be given for the mother to carry the baby to full term and the deeper that the mother can relax herself the longer the baby will be able to relax and wait till it is the natural time for the baby to be born.

Tell the mother that the pain will only feel like pressure. That there are three ways that she can accomplish painless childbirth such as misdirection of attention by focusing on being at their safe comfortable place, the wrist squeeze method, and glove anesthesia.

I suggest that the patient count the number of breaths between contractions. After doing this two times to add the number and divide them by two. Then to repeat this. Their husband or coach can help them keep track of this.

As they do this they will go deeper and deeper relaxed and will then notice that the breaths become less and less between labor contractions. This shows that the labor is progressing nicely and that they are releasing more each time.

Wrist squeezing method for husband or coach: gently squeeze the wrist and suggest, "As the pressure on your wrist decreases you will be able to go more relaxed and feel only pressure with every contraction". Repeat this suggestion between labor contractions as well as during them.

When they practice the techniques during the pregnancy the husband or coach should say, "AS I GENTLY SQUEEZE YOUR WRIST YOU ARE ALLOWING YOURSELF TO GO DEEPER AND DEEPER RELAXED. LET ALL THE TENSION LEAVE THE CHEST AREA AS YOU BREATHE IN DEEPLY AND EXHALE SLOWLY. YOU BREATH IN PURE CLEAN AIR AND RELAXATION AND AS YOU EXHALE, ALL THE TENSION IS LEAVING YOUR BODY. AS I LET GO OF YOUR WRIST YOU FIND YOURSELF GOING DEEPER AND DEEPER RELAXED."

Before the delivery, glove anesthesia can provide analgesia to the perineal area. Not all patients can achieve a total feeling of numbness. Therefore, a local anesthetic should be given prior to an episiotomy.

Post-partum contractions and enhancing the healing of perineum tissue can be alleviate the discomfort with Glove anesthesia technique along with end result imagery.

The treatment of toxic hyperemisis gravidarum (morning sickness) with hypnotherapy is contraindicated. Hyperemisis gravidarum that has a pschogenic basis can be alleviated with hypnotherapy.

Therapeutic suggestions for hyperemisis gravidarum should be directed for the relief of tension and anxiety. Self-hypnosis and Glove anesthesia can be employed to ameliorate (alleviate) this symptom.

Safe place imagery and Glove anesthesia can be used to alleviate lower back and leg discomfort associated with physiological changes that take place during pregnancy. These changes are part of but not limited to the position of the fetus inside the mother's womb.

After delivery, lactation problems can be alleviated with hypnosis. During the six sessions of training suggestions should always be given for the milk to come in on the second day if breast feeding. That the breasts will be full of good, healthy milk, flowing normally and naturally from the breasts for the baby.

SCRIPT FOR PAINLESS CHILDBIRTH

A CD could be made of this as a re-enforcement for the
mother to listen to two or three times a week.

Teach the mother to be able to do self hypnosis to finally be able to Anesthestis themselves. Tell them to practise hypnosis at least twice a day because, everytime they are hypnotized they will be able to go deeper faster. Program them under hypnosis when they are in a very deep state that they can ask their subconscious mind to raise a finger to let them know when their body is in the state of Anesthesia and will feel no pain. Ask them what finger they want to go up to tell them.

Do the Somnambulism and Esdaile Coma State Induction then say the following script.

YOUR BODY FEELS GOOD, IT FEELS GREAT, IT FEELS WONDERFUL IN EVERY WAY. WITH EVERY BREATH AND SOUND THAT YOU HEAR YOU FEEL MORE AND MORE RELAXED, CALM, AND COMFORTABLE.

YOU HAVE A HEALTHY BODY AND YOUR DOCTOR THAT IS WORKING WITH YOU TO HAVE THIS WONDERFUL BABY IS VERY QUALIFIED. YOU KNOW YOU ARE THEREFORE IN GOOD HANDS AT ALL TIMES.

YOUR DOCTOR AND HOSPITAL STAFE THAT WILL BE ASSISTING YOU WHEN YOU GIVE BIRTH HAVE YOUR AND YOUR BABIES BEST INTEREST AND WELL BEING AT HEART. YOU FEEL WELL ASSURED THAT YOU HAVE THE BEST OF CARE.

HAVING THE BABY IS A GREAT BLESSING AND EXCITING EVENT. YOU ARE LOOKING FORWARD TO IT, SO YOU CAN FINALLY HOLD THE BABY IN YOUR ARMS AND LOVE IT.

IT IS ONE OF THE MOST JOYFUL EVENTS ESPECIALLY SINCE IT WILL BE SO COMFORTABLE FOR YOU TO HAVE THIS BABY WITHOUT ANY DISCOMFORT. YOU WILL ONLY HAVE COMFORTABLE FEELINGS.

YOUR BODY IS SO RELAXED WHEN YOU GO INTO LABOR THAT THE DELIVERY WILL BE QUICK AND COMFORTABLE. THE MORE RELAXED YOU WILL BE THE FASTER AND MORE COMFORTABLE THE BIRTH WILL BE.

YOU WILL FEEL GREAT, YOU WILL FEEL, COMFORTABLE, YOU WILL FEEL MARVELOUS IN EVERY WAY.

YOU KNOW THAT YOU HAVE LEARNED VERY WELL HOW TO RELAX YOUR BODY SO THERE WILL ONLY BE COMFORTABLE FEELINGS WHEN YOU GO INTO LABOR

AND DELIVER THE BABY. YOU MIGHT FEEL SOME PREASURE, BUT IT WILL BE COMFORTABLE TO YOU.

NOW WHEN YOU FEEL READY YOU CAN COUNT FROM ONE TO FIVE AND ONLY IN THE FUTURE WHEN YOU COUNT FROM ONE TO FIVE WILL YOU BE OUT OF HYPNOSIS TOTALLY.

GLOVE ANESTHESIA

(If they are not deep enough in Somnabulism so they lifted up their arms and legs, and opened their eyes, they would feel pain unless you do and say the following:)

I'M GOING TO STROKE YOUR LEFT/RIGHT HAND. WITH EVERY STROKE YOUR HAND GETS NUMER AND NUMER, NUMBER AND NUMBER. SO IT WILL FEEL ONLY GOOD COMFORTABLE FEELINGS.

(Slowly start to pinch the fleshy part of their skin between between the base of their thumb and index finger with <u>your finger nails</u> of your thumb and index finger till you are pinching it hard. Don't let go. Now as you are still pinching raise their hand up to their eyes with your other hand and say,)

NOW OPEN YOUR EYES AND YOU WILL SEE HOW HARD I PINCHED YOU WITH MY FINGER NAILS. YOU'R HAND IS IN A STATE OF ANESTHESIA SO IT DIDN'T FEEL ANY DISCOMFORT. NOW YOU SEE YOU ARE IN A STATE OF HYPNOSIS OR THIS WOULD HAVE HURT. (let go now of the pinch so they can see).

(Now program them to be able to do glove anesthesia so they can transfer it to any part of their body.)

ANY TIME YOU WISH TO GIVE YOURSELF GLOVE ANESTHESIA ALL YOU HAVE TO DO IS LOOK AT YOUR HAND AND SAY, "HAND BE NUMB" THREE TIMES AND IT WILL BE NUMB LIKE IT IS NOW. THEN YOU CAN TRANSFER IT TO ANY PART OF YOUR BODY YOU WANT TO BE NUMB. TRY IT NOW. PUT YOUR HAND ON YOUR CHECK AND THINK IT TO GO INTO YOUR CHECK. NOW TEST YOUR CHECK BY PINCHING IT. ALSO TEST YOUR GUM INSIDE AND YOU WILL SEE IT IS ALSO NUMB. (As they do this say,) IT'S NUMB ISN'T IT?

WHEN YOU WANT IT TO GO AWAY JUST THINK IT AWAY. OR YOU CAN TRANSFER IT BACK INTO YOUR HAND AND THINK IT TO ANOTHER SPOT OR TELL IT TO GO AWAY. YOU CONTROL IT BY THOUGHT.

DISSOCIATION AND DISORIENTATION TECHNIQUE FROM PAIN SCRIPT

Dissociation – being in another place,: ex: IMAGIN YOUR ARM NO LONGER PART OF YOUR BODY. Since the body cannot think it will then feel no pain.

Disorientation technique suggestions can guide the patient to another place and time. First the numbers on the calendar, then the days and finally the name of the month are suggested to disappear. When the calendar page is blank, suggest to the patient that they are now in another place and time and protected from harm or discomfort.

The therapist may also suggest to the patient that they are picturing and imagining a large bold face clock with easy to read numbers. The patient is then instructed to imagine all the numbers on the clock disappearing. When the clock face is blank, suggest to the patient that they are in another place and time and free of any discomfort or unpleasant sensations.

ADDITIONAL BOOKS AVAILABLE

These can be found to order by going to the website www.mtiofh.com

Volume I
Instruction Manual
Regression Therapy

This book also has step by step instructions how to guide the client after hypnotizing them back to the events that are causing their problems. Then how to properly do the techniques to resolve the negative emotions from those events so they will no longer cause the problem. It is important to study this entire book before attempting to do this. It is advisable to have had some training in this first before attempting this. "There is much more covered in the book."

To order book contact: Xlibris Corporation, 1-888-795-4274, www.Xlibris.com, Orders@Xlibris.ccom

Class #101 is available on DVD teaching everything in this book.
$260.00 plus $7.50 shipping, insurance, and handling charges (in the U.S.A.)

Volume II
ANALYTICAL REGRESSION THERAPY
Using Finger signals or Kinesiology (Arm muscle testing)

This book also has step by step instructions with scripts of what yes and no questions to ask to regress the client to the events that have caused their problem and what to say to guide them to resolve the negative feelings and emotions so they no longer will have the problems. This is a very gentle technique and faster, because the majority of the time they will have no idea what their subconscious mind is working on. This eliminating and trauma they might have experienced. It is especially helpful when you are working on people who have been very traumatized or abused. It is also very private because the client does not have to describe the incidents even if they do know what their subconscious has regressed back to. This also will get to incidents that are so buried that the usual hypnotherapy would not uncover. "This is only some of the highlights that are covered in the book.)

$16.95 plus $1.02 tax $5.50 shipping, insurance, and handling. (in the U.S.A.)

Class #102 is available on DVD teaching everything in this book.
$1,450.00 plus $9.50 shipping, insurance, and handling charges (in the U.S.A.)

HYPNOSIS CDs for different problems are available. See the website www.mtiofh.com

Printed in the United States
By Bookmasters